SEVEN RADICAL ELDERS

NML NEW MONASTIC LIBRARY
Resources for Radical Discipleship

For over a millennium, if Christians wanted to read theology, practice Christian spirituality, or study the Bible, they went to the monastery to do so. There, people who inhabited the tradition and prayed the prayers of the church also copied manuscripts and offered fresh reflections about living the gospel in a new era. Two thousand years after the birth of the church, a new monastic movement is stirring in North America. In keeping with ancient tradition, new monastics study the classics of Christian reflection and are beginning to offer some reflections for a new era. The New Monastic Library includes reflections from new monastics as well as classic monastic resources unavailable elsewhere.

Series Editor: C. Christopher Smith

SELECT TITLES FROM THE SERIES:

VOL. 4: *"Follow Me": A History of Christian Intentionality*
by Ivan J. Kauffman

VOL. 5: *Longing for Spring: A New Vision for Wesleyan Community*
by Elaine A. Heath and Scott T. Kisker

VOL. 6: *Living Faithfully in a Fragmented World, Second Edition: From* After Virtue *to a New Monasticism*
by Jonathan R. Wilson

VOL. 7: *Plunging into the Kingdom Way: Practicing the Shared Strokes of Community, Hospitality, Justice, and Confession*
by Tim Dickau

VOL. 8: *Against the Tide, Towards the Kingdom*
by Jenny and Justin Duckworth

VOL. 9: *Thomas Merton: Twentieth-Century Wisdom for Twenty-First-Century Living*
by Paul R. Dekar

VOL. 10: *Being Church: Reflections on How to Live as the People of God*
by John F. Alexander

VOL. 11: *A Glimpse of the Kingdom in Academia: Academic Formation as Radical Discipleship*
by Irene Alexander

VOL. 12: *Reforming the Monastery: Protestant Theologies of the Religious Life*
by Greg Peters

VOL. 13: *Fresh Wind Blowing: Living in God's New Pentecost*
by Steve Harper

SEVEN RADICAL ELDERS

How Refugees from a Civil-Rights-Era Storefront Church Energized the Christian Community Movement

AN ORAL HISTORY

Edited by
DAVID JANZEN

with Interviewers
TIFFANY UDOH, KYLE MABB, AND JOHN BETTEN

Foreword by
C. CHRISTOPHER SMITH

CASCADE *Books* • Eugene, Oregon

SEVEN RADICAL ELDERS
How Refugees from a Civil-Rights-Era Storefront Church Energized the Christian Community Movement: An Oral History

New Monastic Library 14

Copyright © 2020 David Janzen. All rights reserved. Except for brief quotations in critical publications or reviews, no part of this book may be reproduced in any manner without prior written permission from the publisher. Write: Permissions, Wipf and Stock Publishers, 199 W. 8th Ave., Suite 3, Eugene, OR 97401.

Cascade Books
An Imprint of Wipf and Stock Publishers
199 W. 8th Ave., Suite 3
Eugene, OR 97401

www.wipfandstock.com

PAPERBACK ISBN: 978-1-7252-5683-5
HARDCOVER ISBN: 978-1-7252-5684-2
EBOOK ISBN: 978-1-7252-5685-9

Cataloguing-in-Publication data:

Names: Janzen, David, editor. | C. Christopher Smith, foreword.

Title: Seven radical elders : how refugees from a civil-rights-era storefront church energized the christian community movement / David Janzen.

Description: Eugene, OR : Cascade Books, 2020 | Series: New Monastic Library 14 | Includes bibliographical references.

Identifiers: ISBN 978-1-7252-5683-5 (paperback) | ISBN 978-1-7252-5684-2 (hardcover) | ISBN 978-1-7252-5685-9 (ebook)

Subjects: LCSH: Reba Place Fellowship (Evanston and Chicago, Illinois). | Mennonites—History. | Anabaptists—History. | Church work—Mennonites. | Church work—Anabaptists. | Discipling (Christianity). | Mennonites—North America. | Anabaptists—North America.

Classification: BX8119.N66 J36 2020 (print) | BX8119.N66 J36 (ebook)

Manufactured in the U.S.A.   OCTOBER 12, 2020

Contents

Foreword by C. Christopher Smith vii
Introduction by David Janzen xi

1. Julius Belser: Toolbox-Toting Visionary of Interracial Community 1
   WITNESSES: *David Janzen, Ellen Butkus, Kyle Mabb, Anne Stewart*

2. Peggy Eberly Belser: Feisty Helpmeet and Peaceable Host 33
   WITNESSES: *David Hovde, Carol Steiner*

3. Hilda Carper: Loyal Truth-Teller,
   Artist of Community, Sister to the Least 59
   WITNESSES: *Sally Schreiner Youngquist, Tatiana Fajardo-Heflin*

4. Margaret Wenger Gale: Divinely Appointed Community Leader,
   Despite Herself 81
   WITNESSES: *Sarah Foss, Mark and Louise Stahnke*

5. Albert Steiner: Geek (before There Were Geeks)
   with a Heart for God and His Nation 99
   WITNESSES: *Jeanne Howe, Bill Castle*

6. Allan Howe: Many Gifts Communally Forged
   into Christlike Service 120
   WITNESSES: *Josh McCallister, Greg Clark, David Janzen*

7. Jeanne Casner Howe: How the March on Selma Moved One Sister to
   Leave Curlers behind and Become a Grateful, Lifelong, Simple-Life
   Servant of Jesus in Community 149
   WITNESSES: *Linda Kelsey, Heather Ashcroft Clark*

8. Concluding Reflections: Priceless Treasure in Cracked Pots 168
   —David Janzen

Appendix: A Brief Chronology of the Seven Radical Elders' Story 185

Foreword

C. Christopher Smith

MANY IDEALISTIC YOUNG PEOPLE see the injustice and hypocrisy of conventional society and act to make bold changes, but soon they flame out in discouragement or revert in disillusionment to the status quo. By contrast, this is a book of prophetic lifelong testimonies, stories about the radical loving-kindness of God poured out upon creation through seven particular persons and three particular communities. The stories ultimately converge at Reba Place Fellowship, an intentional Christian community in Evanston, Illinois. But before I suggest why you, the reader, should pay careful attention to these brief memoirs, allow me to share a testimony of my own.

I grew up on the fringes of Mennonite culture. My parents are both graduates of Goshen College, but I grew up in an area without any local Mennonite congregations, so I've never myself been part of a Mennonite church. I first heard of Reba Place Fellowship as a young child in the early 1980s through some Mennonite publication, either telling their story or encouraging readers to lift them up in prayer. Somehow, the name of Reba Place stuck with me over the years, lingering as a rudimentary sense of the possibility of following Jesus in intentional community.

It was not until 2001, when I was newly married and exploring the possibility of living in an intentional Christian community in Ohio, that I came to visit Reba Place for the first time. My wife, Jeni, and I stayed at the Clearing, the household led in those days by Julius and Peggy Belser. We were fortunate to have extended conversations with them over meals and experienced firsthand community life in their corner of Evanston. Over the last two decades, I have stayed many times in the Reba Place community, usually assigned to stay at the Clearing. I have been shaped by the Belsers' hospitality and their gracious practices of conversation. They were ever curious about me and the community to which I belonged, and inspired me with their deep commitment to following Jesus with the particular people of their community and neighborhood.

Likewise, I was privileged to know Allan Howe over the last fifteen years, until his death in 2019. Allan (along with David Janzen) was a rich source of wisdom about urban community development that has blessed us at Englewood Christian Church in our own expanding ministry. Allan also inspired me to study the history of the monastic tradition within Christianity in order to understand the challenges and opportunities of life in Christian intentional community. Indeed, without Allan's gentle nudging, I might not have found myself as series editor for this series of books on New Monasticism, or even to be writing this foreword.

My experiences with Reba Place over the last two decades have confirmed for me the truth and the wisdom inherent in the stories of this book. Reba Place has offered and continues to offer a richly formed imagination for Christian congregations and communities that want to cultivate a deeper common life among themselves and with their neighbors as a radical alternative to the conventional wisdom of a self-seeking and contentious world. Every facet of their lives is shaped by the conviction that we have been created as social beings and called in Christ to intimate, everyday community with other Christians who inhabit our place. The threads in the tapestry of Reba Place's history that you will discover here do not idealize the life of daily, intentional Christian community. You will encounter many economic, racial, and relational struggles these leaders faced. But what I find compelling about these stories is how these leaders kept growing in Christian character in the supportive context of long-term friendships in community. In the vast loneliness of the twenty-first century these stories help us imagine a distinctively Christian way of life in which we have faithful companions growing with us in maturity of character through the struggles of a common life.

This volume is not only a rich well of narrative wisdom about life in Christian community, it is striking in the way it portrays the history of this particular community. The history of Christianity is usually told in two divergent ways: either elevating heroic stories of individual saints (which diminishes the social networks in which they were embedded) or looking broadly at social movements (without enough attention to the personal gifts, devotion, and struggles of those within such movements). In *Seven Radical Elders*, we find a careful narration that holds together these two

Foreword

extremes and that pays honor both to these seven saints and to the local Christian community in which they were embedded together.

The apostle Paul's metaphor of the church as a body has long been fascinating to me. Any particular part of the human body makes no sense without the body as a whole, and a body could not function apart from all the particular parts that comprise it. In this book, we get a vibrant depiction of the body of Reba Place as a whole, fleshed out in the stories told by each of these seven elders, along with testimonies of the faith of these elders by other members of the Reba Place community. Stories like these remind us of where we have been and help us discern how God might want to keep growing us in faithful Christian witness.

I encourage you, as you read this courageous book, to pay attention to how its stories are told. As one who is often called upon to tell the story of my own congregation, and who also equips other congregations to reflect on and tell their stories, I was deeply moved by the way in which these stories are told, which affirms the lives of both the elders and the community as a whole. In a culture in which the social fabric is long past threadbare, the care we exercise as churches in telling our stories in this manner could open rich possibilities for cultivating community in society as a whole, honoring personal commitment, and celebrating the shared life without which we cannot flourish.

Whatever sort of faith community you find yourself in, a traditional congregation, an intentional community, or even perhaps a monastic community, these stories will stir your imagination for how your own community can tiptoe faithfully into a deeper shared life. I know that my own imagination has been awakened and that the wisdom of these stories will blend into the conversations that my own community has about the shape of our life together.

4 September 2020

C. CHRISTOPHER SMITH is the series editor for the New Monastic Library, the founding editor of *The Englewood Review of Books*, and author of several books including, most recently, *How the Body of Christ Talks: Reclaiming the Practice of Conversation in the Church*. He is a member of the Englewood Christian Church community of the urban Near Eastside of Indianapolis.

Introduction

*Historical Context, an A-B-C Kind of Life,
and How This Book Was Built*

DAVID JANZEN

Ever since Jesus set the world on fire with the incarnate wisdom of God, movements of spiritual and social renewal have repeatedly responded to his call with radical alternatives to the corruption, violence, and fragmentation of the wider society. These movements have often given birth to new history-challenging monastic communities, fresh experiments in the truth of the gospel lived out in communities uniquely fitted for the needs of a new time.

In the last generation, many such prophetic and revolutionary experiments have come together under the label of "a New Monasticism." Wipf and Stock's New Monasticism Series has gathered these stories of social and ecclesial experiments along with their fresh reflections on the gospel and its application for our age and place within imperial America.

The "seven radical elders" whose memoirs are gathered in this book were "doing it" a couple of generations before the "New Monasticism" label became current, but their stories belong in this series because their faithful witness has been a guiding light offering inspirational friendships and encouragement for many who followed in the movement. These seven radical elders are a living testimony that gospel-inspired idealism put into action, though it passes through the fire of disillusionment, can result in durable communities of Christlike wisdom.

What do we mean when we say these elders were "radical"? Certainly, they stick out from the mainstream in America by their commitment to

Introduction

sharing possessions and income, making life decisions communally, and living below their means. In these and other ways they were unconventional, even extreme. Yet there is something more profound at work here than just being different. The Latin origin of "radical" is *radix*, meaning "root"—like a radish. A radical approach goes to the root of an issue, down to what is most essential. In this sense, Jesus and his community were radical. Jesus looked past the conventions and battles of his day to address each person's relationship to a self-sacrificing God who calls them (and us) to a radical social vision concerning money, power, and care for the forgotten people living among them. His life with others opened a path of communal resistance to structures and powers that obstruct the coming of God's kingdom. Jesus is radical in a way that keeps addressing the injustices and violence of every generation since. Likewise, the seven radical elders featured in this book present a clear and prophetic critique of the present age coupled with a positive witness to the reconciling love of God in community. Their witness was in no way perfect, but it persisted in radical dedication, learning from its mistakes, faithful to it to the end.

But don't take our word for it. Read on and see for yourself if selling all to buy the "pearl of great price" (Matt 13:46) is a good investment. Is following Jesus in discipleship communities in a life shared with the poor worthy of a life's devotion?

In what follows, we want to contrast two life journeys that begin looking the same but end up radically different. In the church in America, there is a well-trodden path of independent-minded young White women and men who break out of their culture of origin and explore a commitment to the gospel with its radical implications for justice and peace in the world. Their fire may have been lit by a year or two of voluntary service, a mission year overseas, or some other experience that jolted them out of their comfort zone and gave them a vision for building a new world. But their adult efforts to sustain such a life as isolated individuals or as couples alongside the demands of providing for a family and its rising expectations, soon strip them of what the world calls "illusions." Thereupon, they become more "realistic" in their middle years, learning as professionals how to use their privileges to work the systems of mammon so that in their old age they can retire as early and as self-sufficiently as their accumulated wealth allows, and not be dependent on family or community. Through their years they might experience of a sense of community here and there, they might contribute to radical causes and savor nostalgic memories of when they

INTRODUCTION

had more freedom to give their days to those most in need. But their life trajectory basically follows the motifs of A—B—A. Many leave the church because it lacks the power to make a real difference in their lives.

This book contains seven counternarratives that flow upstream against that conventional wisdom, seven parallel memoirs of young White idealists who somewhat naively jumped into a communal life of sacrificial service in an interracial church on Chicago's West Side ghetto during the civil rights era. For a few years, as part of the West Side Christian Parish, their light shone brightly in innovative programs, close-in fellowship of Blacks and Whites in the storefront Church of Hope on Peoria Street. But by 1966 their intentional community and their storefront congregation came to an end both because of internal burnout and the bulldozers of urban renewal. By the standards of institutional longevity, their seven-year experiment was a "failure." That part of the story is heroic, tragic, and instructive in its own way: a story worth telling, which this book endeavors to do. So far, this story follows the motifs of A—B—?.

However, the radical sequel to that breakdown is more surprising. The "success of that failure," we might say, was a group of transformed disciples of Jesus who continued for five more decades of loyal friendships in a communally-sustained witness to Jesus' reconciling kingdom, offering their experiential wisdom and persistent service to Reba Place Fellowship, its daughter community Plow Creek Fellowship, and far beyond. Now in their late seventies, eighties, and nineties, they leave a legacy for hundreds of spiritual children and grandchildren for whom this book was originally conceived. But their seven bundled memoirs are also instructive for any who are curious about how to communally sustain a radical lifelong witness to the way of Jesus in fruitful and joyful resistance in a world that continues to worship at the altars of militarism, money, self, and White privilege. These stories end up following the motif progression of A—B—C. So, what is the secret, the mystery that makes a radical "C" life possible?

But before we answer that question at the heart of this book, we should briefly review the context and relationships between those communities where these seven radical disciples landed and fruitfully served. Then we will review how this book project was conceived, its purpose, and development. Finally, we will pose a series of questions for the readers to keep in mind while immersing themselves in the seven memoirs—naming themes we will return to in our Concluding Reflections.

Introduction

I. The Brief Shining Light That Was the Church of Hope on Peoria Street on Chicago's West Side

The stories of these "seven radical elders" have seven separate beginnings but their lifelines all converge on Chicago's West Side in the late fifties and early sixties, where Julius and Peggy Belser helped found an interracial church/community under the auspices of the West Side Christian Parish. Here's how Julius tells the story beginning in 1952:

> When I first came to Chicago and to [the Church of the Brethren] seminary, Archie Hargraves, a Black pastor, visited and spoke in chapel. He had a vision of church as community, as a part of the broader city life, engaged with local politics and leadership of the neighborhood. [In my mind] Archie's vision combined Brethren Voluntary Service work and home missions (establishing new congregations). He didn't just want to give stuff out to needy people but wanted the church life and the gospel to be at the center of the ministry. He visualized the church on every block, organizing the community. It sounded so right! I came home that day, after he spoke in chapel, and told Peggy about it and said, "This is it. I want to be a part of this."
>
> Beginning in 1953, I spent two years at the Lawndale Community Church working part-time as my practical work for seminary . . . as part of the West Side Christian Parish, where Archie was a leader. It was his vision to invite the West Side Christian Parish to send young educated adults, such as me, to come help invigorate the church. I was called in to be a minister to teenagers. We established block groups, and we used the basement of our church to hold dances. With Archie as the pastor, the church become very active and vital in Lawndale.

After a couple of years working under Archie Hargraves, Julius had something more radical in mind:

> We had cell groups on various blocks there and a very active church, but the commitment of the neighborhood ministry was not transferred to the commitment of church membership. There wasn't a place for the layman to be part of the group ministry. So as I looked at that, I wanted to be part of a team where the whole church was committed to ministry, not just the staff.

Julius wrote a pamphlet called "A Seed to Grow," inviting young Christian idealists to join him and Peggy in this venture of an inner-city church

Introduction

community that would cross racial lines just as the New Testament church had brought Jews and Gentiles together in one transformative body. Without using the words, the invitation was an early embodiment of the "three Rs" with which John Perkins later challenged the Christian Community Development Association movement for racial justice and economic development: relocation, redistribution, and reconciliation.

Soon other volunteers arrived to form a team of lay ministers living in intentional Christian community on the same economic (welfare) standard as many of their African-American[1] church-mates from the neighborhood. Julius and Peggy, with their growing family, were mentors and energetic hosts for this growing team of activists and community builders. In this era before the Black Power movement, when Martin Luther King Jr. and his coworkers promoted "racial integration," these White volunteers learned through many culture shocks how they were both out of place and yet graciously welcomed in the interracial community called Church of Hope.

A parade assembles for the dedication of the "Chapel of Hope," an early name for the "Church of Hope" on Peoria Street, Chicago's West Side, founded 1959

1. At the time of the Church of Hope the commonly accepted term in America for persons of African descent was no longer "Colored" or more pejorative epithets, but "Negro," which Martin Luther King Jr. used in his "I Have a Dream" speech. However, by the end of the 1960s the Black Power movement had replaced "Negro" with "Black" in common parlance. After Malcolm X left the Nation of Islam, he preferred to speak of "Afro-Americans." Since then "African American" has become the predominant usage in describing persons of African origins in America today alongside other people of color like Native Americans, Asian Americans, etc. I will use these various terms as seems to fit the historical context, but for more recent decades, I will refer to persons in America of African heritage as "African Americans."

INTRODUCTION

Julius presiding at Church of Hope dedication

A common meal for the persons in community at Church of Hope

INTRODUCTION

A Church of Hope live nativity scene involving countless angels, animals and a truck loaned by a local stone mason

Peoria Street Community meeting

Introduction

Their growing community soon included Hilda Carper, who, after teaching two years in local, mostly Black public schools, joined Julius on staff, wrote children's curriculum for the West Side Christian Parish, and organized a Black children's choir that sang widely in suburban churches and on TV.

Margaret Gale, newly married to David Gale, shared life with other mothers of the community, even as she had four children of her own (including twins) during her years at Church of Hope. David was a printer of Quaker background, working downtown, who often assisted with banners and posters for marches during that civil rights era. (David passed away in 2017 and could not be interviewed for this memoir collection.)

Albert Steiner was a first-generation "geek" who learned to program and manage computers when there were only a handful in the country. He lived in a cold-water flat with other volunteers who assisted in the West Side Christian Parish. Between jobs, Albert tucked in a life-changing trip to Albany, Georgia, where, with a dozen others, he spent five days in jail for the crime of praying on the courthouse steps for an end to segregation.

Jeanne Casner (who married Allan Howe in 1965) taught English in the local Negro high school and volunteered as Sunday school teacher. She participated in the second march from Selma to Montgomery, Alabama, with Martin Luther King Jr. and others. While there, she dramatically threw her curlers into a dumpster, marking the U-turn of a fashion-conscious sorority gal to a simple-lifestyle disciple of Jesus in community with the poor.

Allan Howe, a Stanford-educated conscientious objector, became a community organizer, rallying African-American youth for marches and demonstrations to end segregation. In 1963, he helped organize a marathon overnight bus trip of these same young people to Washington, DC, to hear Martin Luther King Jr. give his "I Have a Dream" speech, and then returned the next night, totally buzzed out with fatigue to their homes on Chicago's West Side.

Over the years the Church of Hope on Chicago's West Side was in a growing relationship with another intentional community in Evanston—Reba Place Fellowship (begun in 1957). Volunteers from Reba came to the West Side to give support, while West Side folks went to Reba for rest and restoration. In 1965 Julius and Peggy's marriage was coming apart over the intensity of Julius's commitments. Their family relocated to Reba Place Fellowship for an emergency sabbatical, which turned out to be a move. In the meantime, Church of Hope struggled on for another year as the

Introduction

neighborhood around it collapsed and houses burned without intervention. By that time the West Side Christian Parish operation had already shut down. The city of Chicago exercised its power of eminent domain and claimed vast areas of the West Side for urban renewal projects, scattering the people whose lives had been centered in Church of Hope on Peoria Street.

By 1966, Reba Place Fellowship had established a thick relationship of visits, personnel exchanges, and material support with Church of Hope on Chicago's Near West Side. Reba considered Church of Hope as a mission partner in a more precarious and threatened interracial context. By the end of 1966, the remaining White members of the Church of Hope (except for Allan and Jeanne Howe) transferred to Reba Place Fellowship. The Black members found other homes, some in the newly built high-rise apartments. By 1968, several square miles around the Church of Hope had been bulldozed to make space for "The Projects," barren concrete ghettos for the poor. And in the neighborhood of the small storefront church where our story began, arose the new University of Illinois, Chicago, campus.

These seven young prophets shared a cross-cultural baptism by holy fire, a radical Christian formation that gave direction to the rest of their lives. The end of Church of Hope did not extinguish their hope in God's kingdom coming together in a prophetic community. They had tasted an all-engaging experience of God's work in community such that, when it ended, they wanted more. The core of this book will be the memoirs of these seven prophets with a few interpretive essays wrapped around to fill out the significance of their five-plus decades of faithful and often revolutionary service sustained from a Christian intentional community base.

These West Sider "refugees" turned out, over time, to be a stalwart core for the following decades at Reba and at Plow Creek Fellowship, Reba's rural daughter community two hours west of Chicago. Reba's emphasis on nurturing strong family life with a Sermon on the Mount ethic, and a sideline of increasing expertise in counseling and inner healing work, complimented the more radical social justice consciousness that the West Side transplants brought to the Reba mix. The marvel of this integration of emphases was constantly negotiated in the leaders' group of Virgil Vogt, John Lehman, and Julius Belser, who served at Reba, with others, for almost four decades, from the seventies till the end of the millennium when a younger generation took over.

Introduction

In 1971, Reba purchased a run-down farm two hours west of Chicago, just outside the village of Tiskilwa, Illinois, and soon sent four families (including David and Margaret Gale with five children) to build up a rural community. Plow Creek became a thriving intentional community living in homes built by David Gale and his team of helpers in the context of gorgeous woods, trails and bottomland fields. Weary urban communitarians often retreated to Plow Creek for renewal and to help with the extensive gardens and truck-farm business in summer time. Plow Creek hosted widely attended Shalom Mission Community camp meetings and conferences on their central meadow. The community of Plow Creek flourished for more than four decades, but in 2017 the remaining elders, depleted by recent deaths, decided to end well and pass on their beloved home in the woods to Hungry World Farm, a new nonprofit with a mission to educate a new generation of seekers in sustainable ways of farming, eating, and caring for God's good earth.

With this brief overview of the social and historical context of these seven memoirs, we now review how this book came to be.

II. The Conception, Purpose, and Development of *Seven Radical Elders*

The impetus for this book arose from repeated advice by Reba Place Fellowship members and friends who observed that the amazingly faithful and long-lived first generation of Reba leaders could pass away at any time, or lose their memories. The wisdom of their life experience would be lost unless someone began to interview them soon. So, the Reba Place Oral History Project began in 2012 with an oversight committee and my willingness to serve as its editor. Reba interns were recruited to do the initial interviews. Tiffany Udoh began to meet with Julius Belser and Hilda Carper to write up their stories. But then Tiffany moved on. Similarly, Kyle Mabb continued and largely completed Julius's story and wrote an appreciative essay included in this book. Meanwhile, other work kept coming ahead of this project for me and the undertaking progressed slowly until Julius Belser spent a few critical days in the hospital in mid-2018 and Allan Howe's mental faculties were declining in what was diagnosed as Lewy body dementia. So, John Betten, a Reba Novice, and I got serious about wrapping up this project and set a deadline to complete the interviews before the end of the year, 2018.

Introduction

At first, we called this the Reba Oral History Project and assumed that we would interview the elders who remained from the first decade or two of Reba's history. That proposal, however, was frustrated because some early Reba leaders were reluctant to share their stories due to privacy of information issues, or they were now living at a far distance. Furthermore, "the first generation of Reba leaders" was a group with fuzzy boundaries, making it hard to decide who should be included and who not. Also, many of these stories had already been told up to 1987, at Reba's thirtieth anniversary, by David Jackson in *Glimpses of Glory*.

Then a breakthrough to our dilemma appeared when we realized that the people most willing to participate in the oral history project all shared a highly formative, radicalizing, and bonding mission experience at Church of Hope before they came to Reba. These volunteers stuck together in a powerful way, persisting through more than five decades of changes until this day when the title "radical elders" fits them well. We should also acknowledge the contribution to the common life and ministry at Church of Hope by other volunteers who stayed for shorter periods of time, such as John and Joanna Lehman, Lois Engelman, Conrad and Martyne Wetzel, Herb and Maureen Klassen, and others with briefer stays too numerous to mention here.

Now a word about the process of collecting these seven memoirs: most of the content was collected through direct interviews. In some cases, the subjects gave us written portions of the text. Of course, editorial composition and paraphrasing was involved, integrating the fragments of many interviews into a continuous narrative. Throughout, we have taken care to preserve the subject's voice as he or she would like the story told, and to gain their approval for the final version. I want to acknowledge John Betten's strong assistance, proofreading, and editorial improvements, supporting this project all the way to the finish line. Sally Youngquist and Heather Clark, other members of the Oral History Project Board, also gave editorial and proofreading support, as well as insightful suggestions to keep the narrative on track.

VI. A Few Questions to Keep in Mind as You Read the Stories of Seven Radical Elders

While reading the seven memoirs that make up the heart of this book, we want to suggest a few questions or themes to keep in mind.

Introduction

1. **On leaving and finding**: Jesus promised his followers that by giving up family and possessions for the kingdom's sake, they would receive back a hundredfold in this life, along with persecutions and life eternal (Mark 10:28–31). What conflicts with family and conventional social expectations did these young idealists face, and how did that pan out?

2. **After disillusionment what remains?** What illusions did these idealists have to shed, and what remained of their original vision? In what ways did they remain radical disciples of Jesus to the end of their days?

3. **On burnout and restoration**: The marriages and the individuals in these memoirs passed through crises of burnout, of over-extended participation in the mission of community. And yet, community was also the environment for healing and the support to discover a more sustainable life that fit their gifts. What accounts for the amazing resilience that can admit mistakes and exhaustion, and yet persist gracefully over seven lifetimes of service?

4. **The racial reconciliation impact of seven radical elders**: Did Julius and Peggy Belser's original vision for interracial community die out at Reba, or was it sustained in other "experiments with truth" that contribute to the practical wisdom of the racial reconciliation movement?

5. **The necessity and the freedom of commitment**: Wendell Berry writes that commitment offers the time we need to learn from our failures and to pursue wisdom. What evidence do these stories offer for that hypothesis?

6. **On becoming who we were meant to be—saints**: The essays of appreciation that follow these memoirs sometimes read like hagiography, like admiring stories of the saints from afar. But we also have realistic portraits of the cracked pots that allow the light of Jesus to shine through in faithful and, sometimes, exemplary lives. Is their pursuit of holiness in community boring and tedious, or is it a pathway to authentic, even eccentric, joy?

We'll pick up this conversation again in our Concluding Reflections.

ONE

Julius Belser

Toolbox-Toting Visionary of Interracial Community

I. GROWING UP

My mom grew up on a farm near Elizabethtown, Pennsylvania. My parents were both the youngest in their families. Mother and Dad met when they were working at Reese's Candy Company. Mother would take a spoon of peanut butter from a hot slab of marble, and then dip it in chocolate and put it in a peanut butter cup. My dad worked at the same factory doing maintenance, fixing all kinds of things.

My dad's family lived in Hershey, across the street from the Reese family. He grew up with the Reese family's twelve kids. The Reese family had an advertisement on the back of their candy box: "Twelve reasons why you should buy Reese's candy" and a picture of their family.

Dad was a skilled tinsmith. My grandfather learned his tinsmith trade in Germany before he came over in the 1880s. My grandfather had a very short temper: he was German. My dad had some of that too. My father grew up in a German Lutheran family. My mother was a devout member of the Church of the Brethren. My dad joined the Church of the Brethren when they got married. At that time, he took off his ruby ring, a ring with a red stone in it. The Church of the Brethren was a plain people, so wearing jewelry was not good.

I was born on March 15, 1931, and for that reason was named Julius, after Julius Caesar who was murdered on "the Ides of March." I was followed by four other siblings, Vernon, Ruth Anne, Jim and John. As the firstborn I grew up feeling over-responsible for whatever happened in our family.

Our family was very concerned that my father might be drafted to fight in World War II. Fortunately, he had started working for the Hinkle Company, making metal tins, sifters, and elevator buckets—"feeding the nation." He and his brother were both skilled sheet metal workers and had previously run their own machinery company. Though he was no longer in business for himself, his work for Hinkle was classified as "high priority," and he was not called to fight in the war.

My mother impressed me with her orientation towards the Bible and prayer: she had a real assurance that God does answer prayer. She'd read to us from *Hurlbut's Story of the Bible for Children*. My mother prayed regularly. She listened to radio preachers and she sent for blessed handkerchiefs from them. So my orientation to prayer and the Bible came heavily from Mother. I came to love God because of my parents.

Dad was a good craftsman who knew how to work hard and have fun. We'd get up on a hot tin roof and work together. After we'd lay out the tin and put it on, the reflection of the sun just came right up in our faces and we'd get a sunburn. We would work together up above the second or third floor and then go down and get a liter of soft drink and really have a nice break. I remember sharing the deep things of my life with Dad while we worked, like telling him that I really wanted to get married to Peggy. I enjoyed working with Dad, and he enjoyed us kids. He had patience with a lot of things, although not as much patience with Mother.

My mother was a fearful, sometimes paranoid person. During the summer, Dad worked hard and accumulated quite a bit of money. During the winter, he didn't have outside work, so his savings were all eaten up. Mother had a lot of desires for things; she and Dad fussed about money and other basics. She was concerned that my dad was interested in other women. It wasn't true but they'd fuss. Eventually, they bought a little farm, four and a half acres out on the top of the hill overlooking Elizabethtown. My parents loved us kids, and they did all they could to care for us.

Growing up, the biggest concern of my life was the conflict between my parents. At twenty years old, I felt helpless and asked for God to intervene in what seemed like a hopeless situation. The level of conflict seemed to increase despite my attempts to help out around the house and ease the strain. I worried about whether they'd separate and get divorced. Finally, I came to a peaceful place, leaving it to God whether they'd stay together or separate. The "Red Sea" experience in my life, the parting of the waters, was when my parents drove down the road to see a counselor, Robert

Eschelman, one of my college teachers who I thought could be helpful for them. It was the answer to years of praying for them.

I've read Karl Lehman's book *The Immanuel Approach* about prayer therapy. In the book, Karl Lehman talks about establishing an anchor to a positive memory that helps you build a positive relationship with God. For me, this memory of my parents leaving to see a counselor is that experience of God's deliverance that I go back to and remember how God led us through it. It wasn't just a personal experience: it was the healing of my family. After that, there were still lots of conflicts between them, but I knew it wasn't the end of their marriage.

Our church was in a very agricultural society, with community and the nitty-gritty of life all bound together. Though we were middle class, our concerns reached beyond our own welfare. The work of the Brethren Voluntary Service was very central in our church life: caring for refugees and sending disaster relief to third-world countries.

Dan West was a very peaceful and successful man in the Church of the Brethren; I knew him personally. He went over to Spain during their civil war, and what he witnessed there turned him off to the whole business of war and, eventually, inspired him to found Heifer International. He inspired me too. In high school, my constant talk about peace and the joy of Christ earned me the nickname "One World Belser." During World War II when others were selling the customary war stamps, I decided to buy Brethren service stamps. Integrating faith, everyday life, and action for justice would become a theme throughout my years.

One of my most special relationships was with Harvey and Violet Kline. Violet was a sister to my mother. I spent my summers on Uncle Harvey's farm near Lebanon, Pennsylvania. I rode a bicycle (two hours) over there one time. We had so many good events in their front yard playing croquet or playing softball. We'd get ice cream on Sunday nights at Zigler's: twenty-five cents a quart of homemade ice cream at special celebration times. My cousin Harvey was a pre-ministerial student. He was ten years older than me and influenced me very strongly. He was my role model.

II. Courtship and Marriage

I met Peggy because she was part of our congregation. In 1948, just after finishing high school, I went with Peggy's family to the Church of the Brethren annual conference in Colorado Springs. During that trip I felt more comfortable with them and with Peggy in particular. I pursued the relationship. Peggy took a year off college to volunteer with Brethren Voluntary Service as part of a "peace caravan" that went to the different churches, championing the peacemaking vision of the Brethren.

I did a little dating when I was just beginning college. Peggy and I were still writing to each other. As it turned out, at one point I had a date with Mary Greenwalt to go to a district Church of the Brethren conference, and Peggy let me know she was coming home that weekend. So, I had to decide [Julius starts laughing] . . . I had to decide just how serious our relationship was. At another time, a Church of the Brethren ministerial student approached me in college, wanting to know how serious I was about Peggy. I made it clear that I was pretty serious. When she came back from her year away, her experiences had introduced her to the Church of the Brethren and its peace witness in a much more radical way. That radical inclination seemed really right to both of us. At a certain point, we had done so many things together, our relationship had quite matured. Peggy graduated a year ahead of me, but she was ready to wait until I finished college. Then I was ready to marry her.

III. Seminary and Community Action in Chicago

I went to the Church of the Brethren Seminary in Chicago because it was the only seminary of our denomination. There I was impressed by a recently returned missionary who lived a life of courage in the Lord, a deep joy that overcame fear. She had been hired as a caretaker for Prime Minister Nehru's children in India. I remember that she had a very bold laugh and was deeply interested in Christian community. Her brother and his family were part of the Society of Brothers, or Bruderhof.

My Bethany classmates and I had already been in considerable dialogue with the Bruderhof about Christian community. One of my classmates, Bob Wagner, visited a Bruderhof community in Paraguay that had fled to escape the Nazis before the War. He came back saying, "This is the closest thing to the New Testament I've ever seen, the way they lived together . . . the way they loved one another." The thrust of that community was very impressive to him. Four couples out of our graduating class left to be a part of Bruderhof communities instead of taking pastorates in local churches. We all visited them, and I was very impressed, but their communities were only located in isolated places like rural New York.

My calling was to start a community like that in the inner city—in Chicago. I thought that the healing power of their community needed to be planted in the raw, sore heart of the city. I was inspired, just the same, and began to consider ways of bringing their presentation of the gospel to the places that needed it the most.

When I first came to Chicago and to seminary, Archie Hargraves, a Black pastor, visited the seminary and spoke in chapel. He had a vision of church as community, as a part of the broader city life, engaged with local politics and leadership of the neighborhood. Archie's vision combined Brethren Voluntary Service work and home missions (establishing new congregations). He didn't just want to give stuff out to needy people but wanted the church life and the gospel to be at the center of the ministry. He visualized the church on every block, organizing the community. It sounded so right! I came home that day, after he spoke in chapel, and told Peggy about it, saying, "This is it. I want to be a part of this."

Beginning in 1953, I spent two years at the Lawndale Community Church working part-time as my practical work for seminary. This was a Presbyterian congregation with only a handful of mostly White members left (about eight or ten of them). The West Side Christian Parish, where Archie was a leader, gave some money to revitalize this congregation that was in a neighborhood that had just gone from total White to total Negro in five years. The whole neighborhood was in turmoil. The Presbytery invited the West Side Christian Parish to take charge of the church. The Parish assigned Archie Hargraves as pastor. It was his vision to invite the West Side Christian Parish to send young educated adults, such as me, to come help invigorate the church. I was called in to be minister to teenagers. We established block groups, and we used the basement of our church to hold dances. With Archie as the pastor, the church become very active and vital in Lawndale.

I was particularly concerned about jobs for the teenagers. A pastor in Ohio found out that the local farmers needed help with their crops. I guess it was the corn. I loaded up a big school bus with twenty-five teenagers, young guys who were willing to come and work and earn some money. It all fit together, I thought. These guys were eager to get going; they were looking forward to getting some money. The problem came when we got there and looked at the living facilities. These shacks that they would live in were pretty bad. The young guys said, "We're not going to live here." The farmer had housed migrant workers there previously, I guess. The pastor didn't think about if these facilities were livable. His expectations were unreal. I felt that we had done a poor job of investigating. The pastor was apologetic, he took us into a restaurant in town and we had a meal. Then we loaded up and headed back to Chicago. That was one difficult experience. Nevertheless, when we got back to Chicago we loaded the bus with watermelons and sold them up and down the street. Selling things door-to-door was pretty common in that neighborhood.

As I graduated from seminary, I reviewed our experience of these two years in Lawndale. My basic sense was that we had established a very active Black church but it wasn't the life together that I was hoping for. We had cell groups on various blocks there and a very active congregation, but the commitment of the neighborhood ministry was not transferred to the commitment of church membership. There wasn't a place for the layman to be part of the group ministry. So as I looked at that, I wanted to be part of a team where the whole church was committed to ministry, not just the staff.

IV. Church of Hope on Peoria Street

After I graduated from Bethany Seminary, the West Side Christian Parish invited me to begin a new ministry in the very blighted Maxwell Street neighborhood. Before moving, I studied the area west of Halsted, north of Thirteenth Street. Originally, it was an Eastern European Jewish neighborhood. Many of our buildings had mezuzahs and were still owned by Jewish landlords. I visited the various storefront churches, the YMCA, and the police station, trying to begin with as much local perspective as possible. At that point, I had written "A Seed to Grow," a proposal to form a little colony of God in the city. It set forth a vision of a life together that had an all-out commitment that involved us and our families. I proposed that we invite young individuals and couples to come be a part of an inner-city ministry where the ministers would be lay professionals: school teachers, businessmen, social workers, and so on. Everyone would commit to being a core member of the church community. The ministry would include all the members of the congregation, not just a few professional ministers. This was the vision for Church of Hope when we got that going.

I invited young people because they often have a reckless readiness for challenge, and I think that's the spirit that Jesus brought. Young people have the freedom to make choices that aren't as complicated as they are in later life. The call wasn't just for young people; I was putting this out to anybody who would catch the vision. I sent that proposal out to college and seminary people, and a few young people came to live with us. Allan Howe was one of those guys; he came to do his service as a conscientious objector in the West Side Christian Parish. Allan gathered the young Black guys and organized them into a civil rights youth movement. Hilda Carper came and taught at a local public school. Albert Steiner came from Goshen College and Conrad Wetzel was a social worker. David Gale was a printer working in the Loop in a print shop, but living in our Project House.

We wanted to live on the same basis as the lower-income people in our church. Some of our neighbors were on public welfare, so our church members agreed to live on the same budget. The rest of the money went to our community and that established a common purse. At that time, our financial discipline inspired Reba Place Fellowship to adopt the same practice of living on the welfare standard.

We first began Church of Hope in 1959 on Chicago's near West Side. We moved into the second floor of a big apartment building, and we tried to fix up the place. Two teenagers, Jessie and Tony, helped us with the move. Jessie was the son of a family across the street and Tony was their friend. Tony said, "Reverend, you got a gun?" I told him that I didn't believe in using a gun. And Jessie said, "That's okay! Tony and I, we'll protect you!" Then Jessie pulled out a .38 revolver on wash-line rope tied onto his belt. They were good guys. But getting into the violence of the street was more than I cared to manage.

A young couple on their honeymoon came to visit us. All their wedding presents were still in their car. However, after their visit, when they returned to their car, all the presents were gone. I went back to our alley and found most of the presents in the gang members' stash and returned them to the young couple. After that we told all our guests to park right in front of our house and make sure folks on the street saw them come into our door. That way their things would be safe.

We got acquainted with neighbors pretty readily through a variety of venues. We shared with people over the back fence and the supper table. We showed movies out of the window of our house. We even built a playground on a vacant lot next door with the help of suburban church kids. While this was happening, I went down to some construction workers excavating for a new highway nearby, and I asked, "Can you bring some fill dirt in for us?" They did, and they even brought a bulldozer to level it. They said, "We're like Robin Hood! We steal from the rich and give to the poor!"

A big area of outreach was to single-parent families, since most of the households in the neighborhood were headed by single mothers. We held a family night once a week, which was sort of a potluck for the single mothers in the area and their families. We even had the local shoeshine man come out and offer his services. We had a very intimate relationship with the young mothers. One mother, Eula, told us, "I have really found something special here. I've been immersed in this new life, and I don't want this guy to ruin it." She worried about her boyfriend, Sunny, who was coming out of jail. Her boyfriend didn't like the community, didn't have any idea about it. One night he came into the third floor of our flat through the back window, and I went up there in my pajamas. I said, "Sunny, you don't belong in here." He could have thrown me off the porch! But he walked down to the first floor and left. Eula became pregnant and tried to hide it for a long time. She decided to leave. I wasn't gifted to take on Satin and Sunny, the boyfriends of these women.

Entering into the life of these young guys and their gang on the street was something I wasn't prepared to do. Archie Hargraves could have done it because he was aggressive. If you gave Archie the Anabaptist vision, I think he could have accomplished it. Herb Klassen could do it; he was a University of Chicago student who was part of our team. He really took on Bill Shumpert (a young Black man) in a brother-to-brother kind of way. But I wasn't able to do that. We could relate to the young mothers and their kids and to some of the older mothers too. But I couldn't relate to the young guys.

Julius on a Church of Hope-sponsored field trip,
acquainting inner-city children with farm life

Julius Belser and neighbors in front of Chapel of Hope

V. Family Struggles and a Sudden Move to Reba Place Fellowship

We had a family of our own to raise. Nevin, our eldest, was born while we were still at Bethany Seminary. Nina was born while I served as interim pastor at First Church of Brethren in Chicago, after seminary. While living on Peoria Street, in a mostly Black neighborhood, Nevin had little trouble interacting with the other children around. Very quickly, he cultivated a lingo of the street and another lingo at home. He went to the local public school and the kids pretty well accepted him. One time he came home crying that his ball had gone over the back fence. He complained that "those White kids" would never give him his ball back. That's how much he identified with the Black kids on our street. Our girls were much more withdrawn while we were on Peoria Street. It was their well-being we had in mind when we decided to send the kids to a local private school.

We had a tough time in general on Peoria Street. The racial tensions all across the United States in the early sixties were very real in our little West Side neighborhood. Lawndale, after all, had been a base of operations for Martin Luther King Jr. in Chicago and his initiatives were coarsely resisted by the police force and Mayor Daley's administration.

At that time my wife and I became overwhelmed while taking care of our infant daughter, Ann, who was born while we lived on Peoria St. She had very small air passages and would throw up most of her milk and food. We prayed for Ann. Eventually, I contracted Mononucleosis. It happened that Ann, Nevin, and I were all in the hospital at the same time. Peggy was so weighed down. There were so many demands on her and so many issues in the neighborhood. Peggy loaded up inwardly. She was unable to express her feelings. She thought if she really shared with me I'd leave by morning. Peggy and I decided that we needed a break.

I should have been more sensitive and open to Peggy. I should have paid more attention to where Peggy was at and been with her more while we were taking care of Ann. Also, I should have been more open to the other members of the West Side Christian Parish about our struggles. Finally, I announced that we were leaving and going to Reba Place Fellowship in Evanston. That was not consensus decision-making.

I left Church of Hope under a cloud of failure. When I came to Reba Place, I struggled with how John Miller evaluated me and my ministry at Church of Hope, which he thought was inadequate. I concluded that he was right. I was inadequate as a pastor and as a leader. I felt I had given all I knew how, and it wasn't enough. For a time I lived with a sense of deep overwhelmed-ness.

VI. Settling Down in Evanston

When we left the West Side Christian Parish in 1965. Reba seemed like the best alternative, even though we didn't see Reba getting very far in addressing what had been our key concerns in ministry: helping broken families and addicted persons. Meanwhile, the city had slated our old neighborhood for "urban renewal" and they bulldozed it to make way for University of Illinois Chicago's Circle Campus, so everyone else was compelled to leave as well.

Life at Reba was good for our kids; they found lots of "aunts" and "uncles." Ann learned to play the guitar from Eunice Mast. Nevin had Carl Helrich as a mentor, who taught all the young guys how to make model airplanes and work on automobiles, learning a lot of enjoyable skills. Nevin even built a crossbow that he tested in our garage—the first arrow went straight through a bale of hay and into the wall! Nina did a lot of sewing; at one point she made the sails for a boat that Russ Harris was restoring. It was difficult for Nina because there weren't any patterns to go off of, but she did it! Russ dubbed the boat "The Nina B" in gratitude for her work.

We had a lot of good times as a family too. When our kids were fourteen, twelve, and ten, we had one of our best vacations ever. We took our bicycles and went on an adventure to Wisconsin, seeking our fortune as we went along with a one-burner stove and a sheet of plastic with rope sewn into the edges for a shelter. Each of us took only a sleeping bag and one change of clothes. We were out for two weeks. We'd often stop at churches and ask to sleep in their front-hall or on their porch.

Eventually, our family moved into a very nice apartment on Elmwood Street. We fixed it up quite a bit, put some color in it. The Howes were next door and the Lehmans were on the first floor, so it was a very communal kind of arrangement. The Howes's kids were good friends with our children. Tom and Betty Roddy's family was a part of our small group then. We joined the Roddys now and again for demonstrations and peace marches. Soon, however, Tom Roddy began to suffer his bipolar illness. He was very gifted, but not in control of himself. That led to some drastic measures.

VII. Life at the Clearing Household

The Roddy family was living at 722 Monroe with nine children. By then, three were away at school. When Tom declined into mental illness, his wife Betty invited our family to come and live with her for support. We had the model of Church of the Redeemer in mind where they developed extended family households to support families who were in transition. Betty Roddy and Hilda Carper went down to Houston and visited some of those households at Church of the Redeemer. We hoped that a similar kind of transformation could happen here. Our children didn't think it was very wise for all of us to live together. Our kids had a lot more wisdom than we did at that point.

Going through those ups and downs with Tom acting out was a very challenging experience. Following the example of the Church of the Redeemer, we trusted the gifts of the Holy Spirit to bring transformation. We urgently prayed for Tom's deliverance and hoped for healing. But that didn't happen. I was responsible to keep the Roddy family safe because, at times,

Tom threatened to harm them. I had Virgil Vogt and John Lehman, other Reba elders, as back up. Eventually, Betty got a legal restraining order to keep Tom away, so if he appeared he could be arrested. Finally, we deemed it necessary to physically restrain Tom and commit him to the Chicago State Hospital. After that we had to attend a series of court hearings to make sure his family was safe. To take charge of a person against their will is a horrendous experience.

We saw ourselves as one extended family household. Betty and Peggy were household leaders. We cared for the Roddy children and cultivated a good relationship with the oldest boys and a girlfriend. Each of the Roddy children are bright and did reasonably well, but after a year and a half together, our relationship with Betty broke down and she moved out.

Tom never received healing and deliverance according to our hopes. But the whole process did result in a deliverance of sorts. Finally, what brought Tom the ability to be sociable was a medication: Lithium. He recognized his need for it and he took it. When he took his medication, he was reasonable. But Betty would not have him back. After Betty and her kids moved out of 722 Monroe, Andrew Lehman, a single fellow, moved in with the Roddy family at 720 Reba Place to give support.

After the Roddys moved out, Peggy and I became leaders at 722 Monroe and named the household "The Clearing." Hilda Carper soon came along to help us. That was a far more realistic way to do hospitality.

VIII. Community Organizing

Back in our Church of Hope days, we got involved in the local political race for alderman. I went down to research the archives in the basement of the *Chicago Tribune*, which really opened my eyes to the way the mob controlled the real estate business in the city. One of the key persons was nominated and elected to office while serving a federal prison sentence. We witnessed a helper who signed for voters and even went in the booth to pull the lever for them. Persons got paid a few dollars for their vote. Our reform candidate, Florence Scala, got only 29 percent of the vote running against the incumbent mob boss, John DeArco. That was a greatly demoralizing experience for us.

Coming out to Reba, we had to think again about what pursuing justice and reconciliation might mean in Evanston. I tried to imagine how we could contribute to the wider community justice scene. A local banker was running for the school board who owned two large apartment complexes in our neighborhood. He ran them essentially as a slumlord until the local newspaper did an exposé on his real estate dealings. Suddenly, he was in quite a hurry to sell them. As a communal church we decided to purchase those apartment buildings and make them available at rates affordable for ourselves and our low-income neighbors.

Reba Place Fellowship did well enough with those and other buildings that, eventually, a neighborhood organization came to us looking for help with another very distressed property on our block at 700-702 Monroe. The place was a hangout for drugs and drug dealers. When there was a shooting on the street in front of the building, I called the alderman about acquiring and redeeming the place and he was quick to work with us. He helped the newly formed Reba Place Development Corporation to acquire state and federal funds and soon we purchased and began renovating the building, which we named "House of Peace."

We had to face the drug dealers and tell them they weren't in charge of this neighborhood, the Lord is! We decided to not renew the leases of a couple of families who let the drug dealers in. But we did it with the support of the alderman and the community leaders. It was a risky step-by-step process. But the neighborhood was glad that we led out in that direction. Reba Place Development Corporation did the same for other buildings in our area. After my experience in Chicago I was glad to learn that this kind of organizing was possible, bringing housing reform in cooperation with city politicians.

As president of the Reba Place Development Corp. board, Julius leads a procession around the House of Peace Co-op building during its dedication in 1996

This put us in the position of trying to be benevolent landlords, working with our neighbors to make redevelopment a reconciling thing. There is, of course, a lot of complexity to issues of power and race when dealing with real estate. We've struggled with how to give renters more power and responsibility in decision-making processes of managing real estate. We resolved to try something different with the House of Peace. The people who lived there were offered the burden and opportunities of being joint owners of the property in a limited-equity co-op. This is still going and seems to be working well, with a lot of our involvement. I served as chairman of the RPDC board from its beginning until a couple of years ago when others were ready to take over.

IX. The Overground Railroad—A Path to Asylum for Central American Refugees

In 1983, we founded the Overground Railroad, recalling the underground railroad to Canada of anti-slavery days, only our operation was legal as soon as we got refugees to apply for asylum. They came fleeing civil wars in places like El Salvador, Guatemala, Nicaragua, only to be sent back to their deaths by the U.S. Immigration and Naturalization Service (INS). It was all over the newspapers back then. I remember thinking about the Mennonite heritage of being refugees who had been chased out of nationalist Germany and Communist Russia, forced to resettle in North America. As once-displaced people, we should be able to understand! Yet it was the Catholic Worker communities that seemed quickest to respond, like Casa Juan Diego in Houston, who hosted refugees without asking about their legal status.

So I made phone calls to find out what we could do about their situation. I called Don Mosley at Jubilee Partners in Comer, Georgia, and discovered that they had already begun to help Central American refugees get to Canada by a legal route. In those days, Canada understood their human rights crisis and welcomed refugees from Central America with a well-founded fear of persecution. Jubilee Partners was organized around a refugee welcome center ministry, receiving and orienting people from Central America going north to Canada.

Then I called the Mennonite Central Committee and talked with Don Sensenig, who was appointed to refugee concerns. I asked MCC if they could support us for the first three months to send somebody down to Texas and interview refugees in the detention camps down there.

I talked with my sister and brother-in-law at Reba who were fluent in Spanish (Ruth Anne less so than Richard) and asked, "Would you be willing to go to Texas for three months and test out this Overground Railroad plan?" With money committed from MCC, and Jubilee Partners willing to take people selected for asylum, they were willing to interview refugees and select the ones in need of protection and willing to live in Canada. That's just what Richard and Ruth Anne were willing to do. With MCC and Jubilee, it seemed like the right thing to do. God was at work in it all.

Jubilee Partners outfitted a school bus to bring back a load of refuges at a time. They had contacts with the Canadian consul in Atlanta. So the plan developed for us to bond refugees out of detention and take them to Jubilee where the Canadian Consul from Atlanta interviewed and accepted them. After six months or so with U.S. host churches, they would be approved to go to Canada. When they left the U.S., their bonds were refunded so the money could be used again. So my vision was to give local churches the opportunity to host and transport these folks until they Canada was ready to accept them.

I sent out invitations to local churches that I had some contacts with and wrote the first issue of a newsletter. We got contributions from all around, from people who knew what it required. At one point, we were thousands of dollars in debt; we had to just reach out and get help to do the job. The Clearing also had quite a few refugees coming and going here. Our guestroom was turned into the Overground Railroad Office.

About this time, David Janzen and his wife came to Reba for a sabbatical. He was an ideal guy to take over leadership of the Overground Railroad. I tried to oversee his work in compiling the newsletter. I discovered that he was so much more capable than I was in writing, and he has administrative gifts. I kept up the relationships with the churches and the neighborhood, while David helped keep refugees moving across the network to host groups that had been oriented to the dangers of arrest. So I worked with him and cared for the people in our household.

One young woman, Mary Jude Postel, with excellent Spanish, came to live in our household. She was recovering from emotional illness and needed a volunteer assignment, so she became David Janzen's assistant. We also had a medical student at the University of Illinois, Eric Bowens, who had spent his summers in Guatemala and was fluent in Spanish. So with such volunteers and occasional refugees as guests, the household was oriented toward this Overground Railroad work. These refugees applied for asylum in the U.S., making them temporarily legal. Eventually they got U.S. asylum or were denied and went to Canada.

We were sometimes under surveillance. It was ten years in prison and a $10,000 fine if you were caught assisting illegal immigrants, but we did it. We brought the Sosa family to Evanston. Eliceo, the father, came first because of death threats for his political activities. He was a good cook in the Clearing and eager to help. But then he found a paying job as an electrician and found his own place.

How Eliceo's family got out of El Salvador was another story in itself. Emma, the mother, was a very resourceful person. Her boys were thirteen and fourteen years old when the army kidnapped them and put them in boot camp. Emma went down to this camp and showed them some English papers insisting that they needed to let these boys go and join their father in the U.S. The camp commander couldn't read it, and in his confusion, Emma hustled her boys out and grabbed the first bus. Then she telephoned us. The Mennonite Central Committee had a representative in San Salvador (Blake Ortman, now at Jubilee Partners) who arranged for these boys to get the papers and the funds to get out of the country. Emma accompanied them to Mexico City first. Then she returned to get her three girls. We had to provide enough money to do this through the MCC representative in El Salvador. Mary Jude and Eric made all the arrangements from the Clearing.

Dan Miller, Hilda's brother-in-law, was a missionary in Mexico City, so we contacted him. He and his wife were ready to host this family that was trying to get out. They arranged for them to get up to the border and cross the river. At the airport in South Texas, the family was arrested and put in detention. The boys had short pants; it was pretty obvious they weren't tourists. Richard and Ruth Anne met them and arranged for a ten-day voluntary departure, because INS had no detention centers for children. They were given ten days to come back for a hearing. We got them up to Chicago where they applied for U.S. asylum.

Here in Chicago, we got good legal counsel for their asylum trial and carefully documented their threat of persecution. All the other previous applications by Salvadorans in Chicago for asylum in the United States were refused; that's why we sent the refugees on to Canada. In the Sosa family trial each person came in separately before the judge and their stories fit together. The Judge said, "I don't know why I'm doing this. But I do believe the story these boys are telling." They "broke the ice." They were the first of many Salvadorans in the Chicago immigration court to be granted asylum in the United States.

Offering sanctuary to the Sosa family was meaningful because it was real. We had a relationship, and this relationship has endured to the present day. The Sosas are our beloved neighbors. One of their sons and a son-in-law work on our property management crew.

At that time, I was one of three senior elders at Reba Place Church. Not everyone in the church or the elders' circle was excited about this refugee ministry, but the other elders were gracious and let me act on my strong convictions.

How should we carry forward this Reba heritage of care for refugees? It's certainly needed in the crisis the Trump Administration has created around asylum seekers. I know that Ruth Anne is not willing to have her tax money used for the military purposes without a protest. But is tax-resistance something we should all do together since we have a common purse? Or should it be more personal? During the Vietnam War, we faced the question of hosting draft resisters and AWOL soldiers. We decided at that point that members were free to act according to their consciences; the Fellowship would support your family if you go to jail. And if there's a ten thousand dollar fine, then fine, we'll deal with that. But we didn't all do it together. So there's a range of different possibilities there. With the Overground Railroad, I just remember feeling so clearly that this was something that I must do.

X. Home Life

Mother and Dad would come out to visit us for Thanksgiving most years. Eventually, they couldn't afford to live by themselves anymore. So our family had a meeting—our kids, my brothers Vernon and John, mother and dad—to decide whether they should move to a Church of the Brethren retirement home twenty miles away or come to live with us here at Reba Place.

Earlier, my brother Jim had broken up his second marriage and was emotionally very shaken. I talked to him on the phone and told him to get on a plane and come out here. He was mentally ill, but we welcomed him to our household. He worked on the crew with Nevin for a time, but Jim was having paranoid schizophrenic breakdowns. Finally, he had an episode where he jumped out the third-floor window of the Evanston YMCA and killed himself. That was very heavy for my parents. But in the aftermath, they experienced the care of the community here in Evanston. So my parents decided to come live with us rather than move to the retirement home. All of their relatives lived in that Eastern Pennsylvania area, and Dad had a business there. But the possibility of coming out here seemed more real after they experienced the care of the community in the aftermath of Jim's death.

They were "Grandpa" and "Grandma" to a lot of people here. Mother and Dad lived for ten years across the street in a garden apartment at 711 Monroe. Dad worked on the crew for a while. When we were renovating the Reba meeting house, Dad worked very closely with Nevin to put in the heating system. He continued working until he developed Parkinson's Disease.

Sharing life wasn't all easy. My mother had problems with her hearing; so, at church, Mother and Dad would sit at the top of the risers to use a sound amplification device. Mother would make loud comments about the people who were coming in the building: "That lady has a funny hairdo" —goofy and insensitive comments. Sometimes I sat near them trying to control all that, but the people who could hear them were very tolerant and gracious.

When my parents needed more help, they lived in our household. Dad was shaky so we built the lift on the porch and to the second floor so they could get to their little apartment. They lived there for five years. Dad died first and then Mother died. When Dad died, Ruth Anne and Richard were in India and couldn't make it to the funeral. When Mother was dying, Ruth Anne and Richard were living in Guatemala, and they got here just as Mother passed away. That was a very special experience.

In this season of life we invest quite a bit of energy in our children. Nina meets with Peggy weekly; I have a Thursday noon luncheon with Nevin just to share time and talk about the problems in our lives. Nevin and Nina watch after our health, and they get more and more involved as we get older. There are times when our primary concern is just keeping the relationships with our children and grandchildren in good order.

XI. Grieving the Divisions We Could Not Reconcile

As I look back over my life one thing that troubles me most is the times when community broke down and we could not reconcile relationships. For many years, I served on a team of three elders. A breakdown came between my two fellow elders over how a complaint against one of them was investigated and not adequately resolved. I tried to mediate a very complex situation but was unsuccessful. The elder under review eventually moved to Kansas with his wife to be near family. The pain continues. It's still an open sore for me. It's so complex that I feel inadequate to jump in and change things. But he does feel my solidarity and considers me an ally. These two elder brothers have talked since then and made some amends but not a full reconciliation.

I was also involved in the case of a complaint of abuse levelled against a leader of another intentional Christian community close to us. I was called in to mediate the incident and to make corrections. After hearing from my colleague, I tried to deal with the incident in a private way—just him and immediate family members. I didn't bring it all out to the light. That proved to be a mistake. Later it came to light that the leader had abused others. His leadership responsibilities were taken from him. The community had other persons with their own history as victims of abuse, so they asked him to leave the community. I felt he had been disciplined in a way that left no redemptive possibility for him to be restored. Eventually, he and his wife moved elsewhere in the state. He was open with the Mennonite Church about his history, and in his last years they received him into membership.

There were other times when my leadership in the Fellowship was questioned strongly. For years I differed from my fellow elders over women being elders or pastors in the church. I thought that if Sally Schreiner, for example, is exercising gifts that other elders are, she ought to be recognized the same way. For fifteen years we went back and forth. We were close to division. But Virgil had a very strong and gracious position—that though we disagree, this is not an appropriate cause for division. Now we have woman pastors and a woman community leader. Sometimes resolving these issues takes a generation, but that is just life.

I'm not of the opinion that divisions are always wrong. Sometimes divisions are necessary. Later, there are also opportunities for coming together: a healing. It's part of the way God works. I don't think it's an ultimate value to stay together no matter what. This is a matter for discernment. But divisions pain me greatly and I feel them to this day.

XII. Looking Back and Looking Ahead

When I look back over my life, there are regrets, of course, but I feel most grateful for my life with Peggy in community. I feel satisfaction in the work we could do with refugees through the Overground Railroad, and for the affordable housing we could offer through Reba Place Development Corporation. A special gift of God's grace has been the people who came together around Peggy, Hilda, and me at the Church of Hope on Chicago's West [Side] sixty years ago, and who have turned out to be friends for life, still with us here at Reba—Hilda, Jeanne and Allan Howe, and Albert Steiner. I worry about what I will suffer if Peggy dies before me. She worries the same about me.

A familiar grin of blessing from Julius the Elder

When I think about death, certain songs come to my mind. "Soon and very soon, we are going to see the King." I make it a practice these days to tell the people around me that I love them. The big thing for Peggy and me is that we're grateful to be alive and still be together. We're grateful for all that's been given.

Julius Belser passed away in his home, surrounded by friends and family, at 10:20 a.m., December 19, 2018. "Precious in the sight of the Lord is the death of his saints" (Ps 116:15).

Advocate, Coworker, Schemer of Good Deeds, and Prophet of God

DAVID JANZEN

I wake up this morning (13 December 2018) with both a heavy and a grateful heart because my compassionate friend, faithful mentor, best advocate, inspired coworker, unstoppable imaginer of new projects to bless the last and the least, this prophet of God for almost nine decades on earth, Julius Besler, is dying. He is going home soon to rest and rejoice with God, leaving us behind. This is no shock. His stooped body more and more often in recent times would fall asleep in mid-conversation, but then his eyes would open and he'd ask us to sing with him, "Soon and very soon, we are going to see the King."

I've been looking over a collection of photos that the family gathered up and shared at Julius and Peggy's sixtieth wedding anniversary. Among them is one with Julius surrounded by a motley crew of mourners and oak trees in the humble Plow Creek Cemetery. There he stands in his lanky frame, slightly bowed, reading from the Bible, presiding at the burial of George Busse. George was a nobody in the world's eyes, someone with limited intelligence, few earthly possessions, mostly abandoned by family, and yet beloved by God, and accompanied in his final hour.

Julius presides at George Busse's funeral in Plow Creek Farm's cemetery, 1988

Here is his body awaiting burial in a finely crafted homemade casket of knotty white pine, a casket with perfect angles and proportions, with dadoed and beveled joints, crafted by Julius and his helpers. Now George's friends are gathered to give him a loving and decent burial. I have joined Julius in building a few other caskets in the Reba Shop, and hope to help his family build a coffin to honor him as he has honored others.

In the early eighties, Julius Belser, one of three elders at the helm of Reba Place Fellowship, was in anguish of spirit. His imagination was seared by images of thousands of Central American refugees fleeing north from death squads and a brutal civil war of the rich against the poor. But instead of welcoming the refugees, the U.S. was sending them back to their deaths and funding their killers. In a Passion Week drama at Reba Place Church, Julius played the role of Pontius Pilate, who turned Jesus over to be tortured and murdered by those who hated him. Pilate then ceremoniously washed his hands of any guilt. In that moment Julius knew prophetic action was called for.

Julius led the way in imagining a network of folks reminiscent of the Underground Railroad, secreting slaves to freedom in Canada. Since the railroad that Julius dreamed up and organized was mostly legal, he called it the Overground Railroad and invited others to join in its operation.

Thirty-four years ago our family moved to Reba and I became Julius Belser's assistant, helping him manage this growing network of churches, intentional communities, and volunteers forming across the U.S. and Canada. Julius had lined up Spanish-speaking recruits to interview those refugees in shelters and detention camps on the southern U.S. border, where they selected those most in need of protection. We'd bond them out of detention and arrange for rides to temporary hosts, communities who could teach them how to survive in "El Norte." Eventually they would land with sponsors in Canada. For a decade we ran this railroad together. He was the imaginative chairman of the board and I was the director. He was the humble stepladder that I climbed to take over his job even as he held me up so I could do my best.

Then when the civil wars in Central America came to an end, we turned our attention to affordable housing needs in Evanston. He was chairman of the board and I was the executive director of Reba Place Development Corporation. That's where I learned that when I knocked on the doors of City Hall, and they learned I worked for Julius Belser, I'd describe the project and they'd ask, "How much money do you need?"

Later, Julius and a few African-American pastors teamed up to organize the Evanston Community Development Association for a similar mission of providing affordable housing in these pastors' neighborhoods. When they learned I was with Julius, I got immediate credibility and welcome. I remember Bishop W. D. C. Williams grabbing my torso with a linebacker's hug and bellowing in my ear, "I love you with the love of Jesus, and there's nothing you can do about it." Then the bishop took me under his wing and coached me on how to use my gifts in service of an organization with mature African-American leadership, moving forward in the wake of my mentor Julius Belser.

I could tell many other stories from our thirty-four years of Monday morning mentor meetings where I mostly talked and Julius listened. Together we hatched schemes that organized many in doing good for the last and the least. Wherever I went, I learned that Julius had already earned the trust that I needed to do my job. Every week Julius would dream up some new community-sized project responding to needs of the poor and oppressed. Then I'd ask, "And who will administer this?" Never dismayed, he would come up with another dream which we'd problem-solve into a viable project. At that point Julius would knock on doors, and because he was

Julius, they would open up. Minority leaders would usually get on board first because they were already Julius's friends.

After three decades of working together in this manner, God provided a coworker, Adrian Willoughby, who now has been meeting with Julius and me every Monday morning in a three-generation mentorship meeting. Two decades ago, Adrian's family, newly arrived from Belize, was struck by tragedy when the father suddenly died, leaving teenaged Adrian as the oldest man in the family. Julius came on the scene, presided at the father's funeral, enveloped the family in his care and problem-solving schemes. Soon we hired young Adrian to help out with moves and apartment renovations so that his family could eventually find a long-term home in the House of Peace Co-op. (That would be another long Julius-inspired story.) And now, two decades later, this descendant of African slaves, Adrian Willoughby, is director of Reba Place Development Corporation, and I am his assistant, trying to do for Adrian what Julius did for me.

There is no end of Julius stories I could tell, but this essay is long enough. Soon it will be time to build Julius's coffin in the traditional Belser pattern. We want to honor his body as his spirit passes on "to see the King" from whom he will surely hear, "Well done, good and faithful servant."

David Janzen and his wife, Joanne, have lived in Christian intentional community since 1971 in Newton, Kansas, and since 1984 at Reba Place Fellowship. At Reba, David has been a coworker and protégé of Julius Belser for thirty-four years.

My Mentor and Friend

ELLEN BUTKUS

Julius, once over six feet tall, now at eighty-seven, with stooped back, barely reaches my shoulder. Even back then his humility kept anyone from feeling he towered over them. Perhaps that humility was the secret to the power of his actions, the success of his projects—one secret, anyway.

The other would be his great heart of compassion, undiminished over the years, that would not allow him to rest until aid or comfort, or justice occurred.

From his thirties through his sixties, Julius was an elder and a visionary leader in Reba Place Fellowship and in Reba Place Church in Evanston. Though his life was complex, Julius lived simply. He was enthusiastically committed to sharing all his goods with others in the Fellowship. His home not only sheltered his wife, Peggy, and their three children, but also many members of their wider spiritual family. Their twelve-person dining table was usually full. Julius and Peggy set the example where everyone took turns cooking, setting table, and serving one another according to their needs and abilities. Their household was named "The Clearing," a place of light and rest in a dark and tangled forest.

The Clearing made room for Guerra, an Angolan refugee whose name means "war" in Portuguese. His name recalled the condition Guerra was born into, what he lived through and suffered before his escape. The Clearing welcomed a grateful single mother, an ex-offender learning how to live free, and it made space for Julius's parents for the last years of their lives. For forty years the Belsers have lived with Bob, a man with quadriplegia from muscular dystrophy, and his caregivers. For a time the Clearing was family for a man whose increasing bipolar madness put them all in need of protection; Julius was first in line to receive his blows and yet grieved when the household insisted he leave. At present, they share life with Julius's widowed sister and seven other housemates.

And Julius mentored me as he established a ministry reaching into homes and hearts of lonely elders in the neighborhood. Julius astutely observed that ministry to elders would be a good fit for my nursing and eldercare background. From the start of grant writing to finding office space and furniture, he brought me alongside, instilling in me the confidence that I could direct such an undertaking. Julius brought in other amazing leaders to support and encourage me. I'm proud and humbled by Julius's guidance that helped me discover this calling on my life. Now twenty-eight years later I am retired, but Senior Connections continues to attract and orient visitors who make friends across the generations.

Julius and Peggy have been married sixty-six years. They count three children, eight grandchildren, and a growing tribe of great-grandchildren. Now I look with wonder at this mighty, mighty, humble man who is bent over because of a bike accident a decade ago, shuffling slowly because of Parkinson's Disease, perhaps not remembering all the great things he has done, but I really think he is bent over from all of us that he has carried on his shoulders.

Ellen Butkus lives in semi-retirement with her husband, Al Butkus, in the Chicago suburb of Oswego, near their two grandsons. For nineteen years she was the director of a Reba Place Church ministry called Senior Connections, orienting and supporting volunteers to befriend and stay connected with elders in the neighborhood. Julius's dream for care for seniors, twenty-seven years later, continues to grow and expand.

Young People Need to Know This Is Possible

KYLE MABB

Talk to anyone who's lived in the Reba neighborhood, and they will surely know Julius Belser. His reputation for hospitality and sacrificial service has made him one of the most visible and memorable members of the community. Likewise, many younger Reba Place folk point to Julius as a source of either direct influence or quiet inspiration. The members of Reba Place Fellowship have diverse perspectives, but all paint the same picture of Julius as a loved spiritual father, universally trusted because of his humble and gentle approach to leadership.

I had the privilege of accumulating hours of interviews with Julius, transcribing and editing the details of his life story, and exploring his contributions that whir at the heart of the Reba Place community today. As we talked, Julius would often make a gesture by touching his thumb to his middle finger in emphasis of the word "real." This might refer to the change the gospel brought to the families of five former alcoholics he met in the hills of Southern Virginia or the sweetness he experienced in leading Church of Hope as a community dedicated to inner city justice and reconciliation. This "realness" has been his consistent pursuit, something he can still touch, a texture of life that drew him out of rural Eastern Pennsylvania and eventually to inner-city Chicago.

Yet Julius is to me more than a paradigm. He stands out as a unique and relevant voice for young Christians who are concerned with kingdom work in two distinct ways. First, at eighty-two years old, he makes no effort to distance himself from mistakes of his past. In spite of Julius's gratefulness for divine providence and the Lord's guidance through trying times, he can still speak about mistakes he made thirty, forty, fifty years ago with sincere regret. I can't say enough about how impactful that was for me. Kingdom work is people work, and intervening for the well-being of others on behalf of Christ can have consequences that go unsaid or underemphasized. Having the clear voice of an elder who does not distance himself from his mistakes and their repercussions is crucial for younger generations to see. Messing up is something that all would-be leaders should get used to, and we should be prepared to follow up with it by practicing the same radical vulnerability as Julius.

At the same time, Julius's resilience is what makes his voice truly powerful. In one of our sessions, he spoke of the tension he often lives in as someone who feels called to Christlike hospitality, and is also responsible for the well-being of his household, family, or community. The hospitableness Julius seeks to embody is the typical Matthew 5 kind, where Christ tells disciples to go the well-cited "extra mile" and "give the shirt off your back" for anyone in need. This verse is speciously upheld by my generation of young Christians. We understand and defend it, but we've created well-constructed rhetorical boundaries that protect us from engaging in a charitableness that has any real cost to ourselves. Our hesitance is understandable: we've seen idealistic and ambitious individuals who wanted to prove that a life of compassionate service and selflessness was possible, only to become overextended, burnt out, and cynical after a few attempts.

Julius's testimony is significant because he does not downplay the difficulty of being immersed in a culture of giving, specifically when it impacts his family and community members, whose well-being he is also accountable for. Nor does he claim that in all his experience has he figured out an easy or formulaic response to people with complex needs. What is instead important is that after decades of complicated interventions and efforts of hospitality, he has not burnt out or given up. He still sees fulfilling the gospel's expectations of giving, sharing, and loving-kindness as his highest pursuits, and at eighty-two years of age he's got the same vigor in him to be a learner-practitioner as any bright-eyed optimist fresh out of seminary. Young Christians need to know that this is possible, that we can pour ourselves out on the altar of Christian service and receive the grace that rejuvenates us again and again. We need to see someone who's made mistakes, gotten burned, hurt others, asked for forgiveness, and above all, kept going.

Julius Belser

The life of Julius Belser puts the terms for our success as socially minded Christians in clear language: that it's going to be difficult, but we can persist; that what we gain is a beauty as enigmatic as it is irresistible; and that the path through is lit by the wisdom of the Spirit.

~

Kyle Mabb was an intern in Reba Place Fellowship's Apprentice Program in 2012–2013. During that time he worked as an interviewer and writer for the RPF Oral History Project. At present he is studying social work in New York City.

Heavy Lifter

Anne Stewart

I asked, "What do you remember and appreciate about Julius?" I was talking to Eloise, an African-American woman, now in her sixties, who, as a young single mother, lived in the Reba Place household called "The Clearing" with her son, Brian, during his elementary and high school years. For decades Julius and Peggy welcomed and cared for a large household of a dozen people that might include more than one "nuclear family" plus several unmarried persons.

Julius and young Brian found an old, broken rocking chair in the alley. In order to teach Brian woodworking skills, how to recognize a "diamond in the rough," and how to make something beautiful with very little money, plus how valuable is a gift that you spend hours making—they repaired and polished this chair for a Christmas gift, and found a way to wrap it too.

Another memory—Brian had a dearly loved pet rabbit named Oreo. Unfortunately, Oreo ingested rat poison and they were unable to save him. Brian was devastated. Julius helped him to build a casket, place his photograph and a carrot inside, and together they conducted a funeral and a burial service.

If you got a flat tire on a bitterly cold day, or if your car stopped on the Expressway, or if the electricity or plumbing failed, you could call Julius. Eloise remembers being frightened because squirrels had gotten into the attic and, of course, Julius took care of it.

A second witness—Dale came to Reba Place in his twenties. His strengths were deep compassion, a solid faith, and a commitment to serve God. Julius was for him a father figure and a mentor. Julius helped Dale to gain the confidence and skills he needed to turn those strengths into action.

But Dale was most grateful for the help and grace his mother, Mildred, received from Julius and Peggy and the household. Since Dale was a primary support person for his disabled mother, Julius and the household cared for her with visits that included house repairs to extend her independence. And when she was no longer able to live alone they took her in to the Clearing Household, where she lived another thirteen years.

Perhaps it is time to state the point of view of this writer. A little background—I moved to Evanston to become a member of Reba Place Fellowship in 1972. I brought with me three young children, ages six, seven, and nine; a broken heart from a recent divorce; dark brown skin and the experiences of a woman of color in the U.S.; some teaching and musical gifts; and my faith. Although I never lived with Julius and Peggy, being a member of the Fellowship and the church meant that I, too, could call on Julius.

"Head of Household" is insider language at Reba and a little hard to translate. Technically, it refers to a person with the authority and responsibility for a very extended family. What it really means, however, is a particular brand of living Christianity that goes way beyond normal expectations. Julius and Peggy gave their lives to this work and it benefited more lives than we can count.

One memory that I treasure—and an example of the practical nature of this kind of Christianity—is moves. A common feature of Reba Place life is moving into or out of houses and apartments. Sometimes there are people moving into the neighborhood to explore intentional community. But because of the value given to the idea that need should determine where you live, there are many internal moves. I don't have any way to prove it, but my guess is that Julius showed up for more of these moves than any other person. For most of those years he used his strength for the heavy furniture. As he aged, a common scene was younger people attempting to discourage him from the "heavy lifting," but with limited success. Perhaps, a person willing to do the heavy lifting is a good metaphor for Julius.

When people talk about Julius's accomplishments, there is frequent reference to far-reaching work like affordable housing and the Overground Railroad, a nation-wide ministry to Central American refugees. I have chosen to focus on the pastor in one-on-one relationships and the practical person who could build and repair because I have such deep respect for this all-day-long everyday service that helped so many of us know that we were not alone. Thank you, Julius.

Anne Stewart is a retired educator and social worker with two decades of experience as an anti-racism trainer. She has been a member of Reba Place Church since the 1960s.

TWO

Peggy Eberly Belser

Feisty Helpmeet and Peaceable Host

I. Growing Up in a Peace-Oriented Church of the Brethren Enclave

I was the first child born to Milton and Barbara Eberly in Elizabethtown, Pennsylvania, in 1929. Elizabethtown was a small farming town on the banks of the Susquehanna River. It was a sort of enclave of the Church of the Brethren denomination. My father came from a family of six-foot-plus farmers, but he only grew to the modest height of 5'5". Nevertheless, he had a vigorous, hard-working attitude. Discouraged from agriculture by his stature, he sought first to be a teacher. Then he reenrolled in college to attain an education in business administration, which culminated in his owning a profitable furniture store. He didn't have any background in furniture so he had to learn a lot. He put in long hours. He and my mother took care of the store for years. That meant we had a lot of family time in the store because the store was just a few steps away from our home. We didn't go away very often because we tended the store. But it was closed on Sundays, like everything else.

My mother was an ambitious self-starter. She came up "the hard way" in a family of meager means, the middle child of eleven. She decided that she was going to go to school beyond eighth grade, so she took a job as a nanny. She used the money she earned to pay for tutoring in Algebra and Latin. Her dad said, "You don't need to go to school to rock a baby." That made her furious! She went on anyway. She took shorthand and bookkeeping and worked in the office of the college that sponsored the academy. In the summer, she went to the ocean and worked in a hotel. The hotel management liked to hire these plain girls with their head coverings because these girls knew how to work. One of the families that she would serve as a waitress liked her a lot and asked her to go with them when the summer was over to Englewood, New Jersey. Mother felt like everything they talked about was very city-like. They took her to the opera once and awhile. She would get into all kinds of things, which was pretty remarkable for a woman in her time. It's probably not a coincidence that Julius is ambitious like that.

My father wasn't very expressive, but he was a generous man and very well thought of. Father would only mark up his furniture for half of what he paid for it, rather than doubling it, which was more customary. After he died, people came and said, "Here's the money he loaned us when we needed it." Father would just take a little piece of paper from his tablet and write a promissory note, and that's all there was to it. No signatures.

My dad got me a pony a little bit bigger than a Shetland, but not like a quarter horse. He said she's lonely, so he built a little barn with a hay loft to house an additional horse. On many Sunday afternoons my father would ride the horse and I rode the pony. That was very bonding. During World War II there was gas rationing, so my dad had a little wagon made with seats and rubber tire wheels. My mother and dad sat on the seat and we children sat with our feet out over the back, and we went to visit neighbors that way.

My parents were also pillars of the church, lay leaders with prominent roles in the congregation. Father was the Sunday school superintendent for many years and a member of the board of trustees. Mother was a choir director. I remember that they were especially attentive to their preparations for teaching Sunday school lessons. As a family, we were sure to kneel together for prayer each morning at the breakfast table, and again before bedtime each night.

If a missionary came to speak at church, we either lodged them or fed them. The food we served wasn't fancy—we didn't know what steaks were— just pot roasts and carrot jello salad, that sort of thing. I remember hosting an exchange student for a year, and we had other short-term students with us through Rotary International. I remember an Indian missionary leader who would visit our church regularly and we always had him over. We had a guest room and we expected to use it; that's where you get some of your broadening experience.

My parents traveled a fair amount for their time. They went to Ecuador to see the mission work of the Church of the Brethren there. They went on a group tour of the historical Brethren churches at the two hundred and fiftieth anniversary of the denomination. The airlines divided the group into two plane loads. My parents came home from Europe in the first group and the second group went down in the ocean near Shannon, Ireland. Five people from Lancaster County perished on that plane. My parents would have been on that flight, but at the last minute, my brother who was twelve years younger decided he would like to go too. So that was probably the reason that he was in the first group and not the second group.

In high school, I experienced a bit of separation from the others. I didn't want to dance or smoke. Many of the girls were interested in boys and I wasn't yet. My pacifist convictions during the War caused me to stand out. I had peers but I wasn't buddy-buddy with them. My parents saw to it that I got my driver's license, but my best friend's mother was suspicious of me and wouldn't let me drive her. She was still my best friend, but she didn't have the same ideas I did.

II. Joining the BVS Peace Caravan

I graduated from high school in 1948. Rather than immediately go to college, I made the unconventional choice to volunteer for a year through Brethren Voluntary Service. Many of my male friends were either being drafted into the military or performing alternative service as conscientious objectors. I had close friends who joined the military, even an uncle, to whom I wrote faithfully. I felt it was my responsibility to do some kind of service as well.

When I entered BVS, we had three months of excellent training. We talked about Tolstoy and Kierkegaard and stuff we never heard about before. As a member of BVS, I was a peace canvasser, traveling throughout Pennsylvania and surrounding states to visit peace churches (Mennonite and Brethren), encouraging them to uphold the traditional Anabaptist stance for peace and non-violence. Even among peace churches there were some disagreements about pacifism. There were families with one son in the army and another serving as a conscientious objector.

For three months, my headquarters were in North Manchester, Indiana. Dan West was there, the founder of Heifer International. He was a lay minister and farmer who worked for peace but without any pay. He farmed oftentimes with a light on his tractor because he was doing his peace work during the day. One evening I went over to Dan's house for supper. Lucy, his wife, was there with their children. I remember seeing an old Persian rug on the floor and it had worn places, and right in the middle of the room was a telescope pointing at the window. I sat on their sofa and the seat collapsed right down to the floor: *baboom*! That was very eye-opening. I had grown up in a furniture store and I thought everyone had nice furniture. In our area, the barns were painted nicely in red with white trim. Everybody had a well-cared-for car kept in a garage. We weren't ostentatious, but it was tidy middle class. But seeing how sacrificially the Wests lived caught my attention.

As we visited churches, we made sure we had a fellow and a girl on each team. Most of the churches we visited were small, especially the rural ones. It wasn't a threatening experience. We went to a church for a week. Most of our conversations were with people one-to-one, sometimes in women's sewing circles, or other small meetings.

Now where it got touchy was in West Virginia and in the Southern states. There we ran into some Primitive Baptists and hard-shelled Baptists, people who were really outspokenly angry about our opposition to the war. They were patriotic. It was a different kind of patriotism in those Southern states. It took courage to say what we really wanted to say. But generally, we were just unpopular, not in any danger.

III. Courtship, Marriage, and Seminary Training with Julius

I don't remember exactly when I first met the most influential person in my life. My parents were designated "visiting members" in the church, charged to visit other families to make sure everyone was reconciled before taking communion. Our family became good friends with a neighboring family, the Belsers, through our role as visiting members. But it was only when I started attending youth group that I came to know Julius Belser. It wasn't love at first sight, but we did have a deep appreciation for each other. Julius stood out as a natural leader with a good sense of humor. He was always thinking of ambitious new ideas. In high school, he was called "One World

Belser" because he believed in a world federation of nations. That was ahead of his time. And he didn't buy war bonds. I was a little shy. I don't know if I talked with him about war bonds or not. Before he could even drive, he organized the town church and the country churches in a softball league. He almost always had a major role in a play in high school or in the church. He wasn't cynical, but very considerate—things I still appreciate about him.

We did everything imaginable together. We didn't just sit around and neck. We washed cars together. We made a solar oven and baked a little cake mix. We wove baskets. We walked a lot. We had a youth group meeting every Sunday evening before the Sunday evening meeting of the whole congregation. We were always together with other youth. After church meetings we'd go to his home. Julius's little brothers and sisters would hang around and say, "Read us a story! Read us a story!" His dad liked me, but his mother thought he should aim higher. My parents thought he was a little reckless. He certainly didn't fit the mold. But they knew him and his family. And then one night his brother called him to come home and go open muskrat traps with him. And I saw his nostrils dilate; he was pretty angry at Vernon for asking him to leave a date to check muskrat traps. Then I knew it was pretty serious between us.

I wanted to finish college before getting married, and I figured that he wanted to finish college too. I was a year and half older, a year ahead of him in college. So it came as a bit of a shock that he wanted to marry me before his last year of college was done. We married in August between his junior and senior years after I was finished with my student teaching. I was only twenty-three when we got married, but we came out of so much of the same culture and even when we didn't quite fit in that culture we were moving in the same direction. It was not that I was so smart or that I knew what I wanted but we had so much to build on. After college, I taught school. In the McCarthy era of communist witch hunts, most work opportunities required signing jingoistic allegiance commitments, something my Anabaptist upbringing made me uncomfortable with. But I was able to avoid the uncomfortable confrontation by working at a school where the principal was a Church of the Brethren minister. So I got the job, and I rode twenty-four miles one way to teach in the school. That was pretty far to commute in those days but the countryside was beautiful and I didn't mind.

After Julius's graduation we accepted an opportunity to move to a small mountain church in rural West Virginia for the summer. Julius was an interim pastor for a congregation while their full-time minister pursued training at Johns Hopkins University. This was our first encounter with extreme poverty, even beyond what the rural poor struggled with in Eastern Pennsylvania. New converts in church would sing with their hymn books upside down. There were few paved roads. A considerable portion of the local economy was supported by bootlegging. Most of the men had been alcoholics, so becoming Christians was a pretty big deal in their lives. Even if they held the hymn books upside down, they knew what being a Christian meant.

IV. Plunging into the Wholly Foreign Urban Environment of Chicago's West Side

In the fall of 1954, we moved to Chicago's West Side. The move wasn't to experience urban ministry or explore solidarity with the poor through pursuing community in the neighborhood; those notions hadn't occurred to us yet. We went there to attend Bethany Seminary, the only Church of the Brethren seminary in the United States. While I taught elementary students in a suburban school, Julius took classes in pursuit of the pastorate. And then First Church was up the block and a half away, which was one of the pillars of the Church of the Brethren.

My parents didn't much like us being in the inner city. My dad said, "Why do people live here stacked on top of each other when there's so much room in the U.S.? And why don't people sweep the porches and gutters, clean up and make the place look better?" They actually offered me money to pay a cleaning lady but I couldn't do that. My mother would cry whenever we would leave on our visits to Pennsylvania and return to Chicago. But they understood that we would continue to make choices that they couldn't understand.

I had taught in Pennsylvania where the students obeyed. When I said, "Sit down," they sat down. When I got out to Chicago, I taught at a new school. The whole neighborhood was new: it was like five hundred homes came out of the ground like mushrooms! We didn't have teaching visuals; the students had to buy their own books; there was no playground, just mud. It was all in a new building with forty-eight new teachers and a new principal. Every morning when I woke it was like having morning sickness—I dreaded going back to that school room. So I called in and told them that I was resigning.

When I became pregnant, I went to have a prenatal x-ray and we learned that I didn't have much room in my hips. It was a very difficult birth. I wasn't prepared with exercises the way they do it now. Baby Nevin was born just before lunch on October 5th. They came back and they said, "You won't be seeing him for eighteen hours." I thought, "Now what's wrong?" Apparently that was the routine, but I didn't know that and I was worried. At the delivery the doctor reportedly said, "That's the last birth of that kind for her." I had a long recovery, which was just part of the whole mess. Nina, my next child, had a much easier birth.

My mother came to help. But she didn't know much about newborns as she had been in a coma a few weeks after I was born, and her other two children were adopted. So, we learned the hard way on some of these things. There was a group of maybe six babies born in a cluster on the seminary campus so I learned from some of the other mothers. But Nevin was a difficult baby. Julius put a hook on the top of the doorway and hung an apple box from it to swing baby Nevin. Julius could study while he pulled the box, and the baby was quiet until he stopped. And then he'd go "WAAAAAHHH." Oh my! He was in agony. Some babies just do this for three weeks, but he didn't straighten out until January. Julius was a youth pastor for his practical experience at Lawndale during that time; he'd come in at twelve o'clock at night and Nevin would still be crying about his seven o'clock feeding. Julius asked, "Did you feed him?" Well, I could have crowned him for that!

At that time, a friend and I traded childcare. I worked at the switchboard at the seminary during the weekends and she would take care of Nevin, taking him wherever she went. She worked during the week and so I took care of her little guy three mornings a week. In her care he settled down. That was a turning point. I thought maybe it was good for him to get away from me because I was so anxious. That's how we got through it.

In seminary, I would go to the playground with all the other young mothers. Julius was very busy, but I felt quite fulfilled. But when he finished seminary, we moved a few blocks away. There I felt a little lonely at times because we had off Monday when everybody else had off Sunday. Across the yard in the next building was my friend Georgia who was Greek Orthodox; that was really a great experience for me because I had always been in a very homogenous Anabaptists setting. The first time I heard her speak, I thought, "Well, I'll never be her friend." She was talking to her kids about something they did that she didn't like and she said, "I'll kill you!" But we did become friends. In fact, she did my hair every Saturday night before Sunday. So when it was going to be Easter Sunday, I told her that I wouldn't come to have my hair fixed up because it's a special and busy day for you. She said, "No, come! You'll mess it up!"

V. We Join the "Group Ministry" of the West Side Christian Parish

After seminary, Julius and I became members of a group of husband–wife teams working with Archie Hargraves and the West Side Christian Parish, which they referred to as the "Group Ministry." Everyone in the ministry was paid according to the number of children they had, according to their need. It wasn't based on the degrees you had or anything like that. It wasn't a common purse, but it leveled things out a bit. We met together for strategy and worship. We had a devotional life; we didn't say how it had to be but you were to spend time in devotions every day. We also had a political discipline. We agreed whom to vote for and whom to promote and so on, so we didn't cancel each other out. It was very different. They all smoked the room gray and I didn't particularly care for that. I didn't like smoking, but Julius said we need to have the ashtrays out and let them smoke. But they were also very devout and just came from a very different angle than we were used to. I respected them very much. When we eventually needed some more help with Church of Hope, they sent us David and Margaret Gale and later Conrad and Martine Wetzel. So we had that association, and also an association with Reba Place Fellowship.

VI. An Interracial Community Gathers at Church of Hope

Hilda Carper had been in Europe and had come to Chicago for a summer institute where Virgil Vogt from Reba was teaching. It was a four-week seminar for people from across the Mennonite Church. Julius had written a little pamphlet called "A Seed to Grow," and somehow Hilda got a hold of it there. That pamphlet is how we met most of the people who came to Church of Hope, and then later moved up to Reba Place with us.

When she first came, she had a room so little the bed was against three walls. That really wasn't adequate for her, so we received money from Reba

Place and bought the house across the street from where we were renting. Hilda moved into the first floor of that building and shared the kitchen with Albert Steiner for a while. When our daughter Ann came along, Hilda would sometimes take her back in her room, lay her on her cot and play with her. She brought music to our kids and lots of creativity. That wasn't my strong point, so I appreciated that. We got along well with her.

When I met Jeanne Casner, she was working with the West Side Christian Parish. She lived in a house in the projects with some volunteers from the Brethren Voluntary Service, just across the street from us. All the people in the house were younger than her, and called her "House Mother," which wasn't very nice.

Jeanne seemed so cosmopolitan. Culturally, I grew up surrounded by the Church of the Brethren and the Mennonites, so I had a rather parochial perspective. I thought everyone ate what we ate—pickled red beet eggs and stuff like that. My acquaintance with literature was lacking. But Jeanne was an English teacher and had all that literary stuff. I was very earthbound, and I noticed that all her shoes and purses matched, and I loved that. She was dressed very smart and chic. So, when she came up to us one day and asked what it takes to join Church of Hope, I thought she was asking for someone else! She was moving in a very different direction from the culture of her childhood. It was very encouraging to have someone like her join us. It was validating.

Rena, a local girl, moved into our housing with her seven children. She had a beauty shop in the little room on the front part of the house. She was on public aid. We couldn't put our finances together with her because the government couldn't handle that, and she feared that we would take her money. But the rest of us—David and Margaret Gale and Albert Steiner—had shared finances. The relationship with Rena, the young mother who lived in the apartment above us, lasted well beyond our move to Evanston. Rena went several years without contacting us, but in the last decades has reached out, even coming to our fiftieth wedding anniversary party. Rena gave us the good news that all of her children had gone on to become competent, independent adults, something she partially attributed to the stability she experienced in the years she lived with us.

Every Tuesday night we had a family night where we went somewhere together in the van. It was usually Rena's children, our children, and maybe one or two other families on the block. I remember we went to see the Coast Guard cutter down by Navy Pier. We went to Grant Park and had a picnic. We did all kinds of things together. A lot of our neighbors would never get out of the ghetto; they were stuck there all the time. Another time, we went up to camp at Crystal Lake at a farm that the Christian Missionary Society had. While camping, there would be three neighborhood kids in three cots at the start of the night. It was dark and quiet, and they couldn't stand it. By morning, all three would be sleeping in one cot!

I tried to build relationships with some of the African-American women on our block and in our church, but it had its limitations. If I came late to a conversation, I couldn't catch up to what they were saying because they spoke with a Southern accent. I got an idea of what they were saying, but it wasn't enough that I could take part. It was almost like going to foreign missions: a different language and a different economic setting. Our neighbors were impoverished in many ways, not just in money. There were no parks. Since we had a playroom, kids came to our house. Our kids didn't go to their house.

I remember I once tried to braid a neighbor girl's hair, only to have it unravel in a few minutes. Similarly, the neighborhood children were infatuated with our children's hair. They would sit on the steps of the building just petting their hair. On one occasion Nevin went for a play date to a neighborhood friend's house and received a spanking from the child's father over some kind of misbehavior. We seldom spanked our children, so they weren't comfortable with an acquaintance doing it flippantly. So we never let Nevin go stay with that friend again. Most parents weren't just unwilling to reciprocate childcare, they simply didn't have the time or space for it. This meant that our dining room was more of a neighborhood playroom.

That was before "Black is beautiful." Our neighbors would treat us politely, but often dismissively. They were willing to accept invitations to church graciously, but seldom would actually act on them. Even with the African-American congregants at Church of Hope, who were more generous in their interactions with us, we still felt these relationships were more limited than what we hoped for. It was only through a few relationships that we maintained after the empowerment many African Americans experienced in the 1960s and 1970s that we could talk more frankly about these things. We came to understand that our neighbors also perceived this rift but didn't trust us enough to address it.

Julius and I faced a lot of struggles in our ministry on Peoria Street. One challenge I see more clearly now is that we were naïve in our expectations of what we might accomplish. We came with the assumption that much of poverty was perpetuated by people who made bad choices out of ignorance and that we simply needed to set a good example of how to live. We learned the hard way that the forces that perpetuated poverty were largely systemic, and if something needed to be relearned it came up against the resistance of hardwired cultural norms. Any change we could actually bring to our neighborhood wouldn't change the overwhelming predicaments of many of our neighbors. It was like putting a Band-Aid on a much wider wound.

**Peggy and Julius on Chicago's West Side with children
Nevin, Nina, and Ann, ca. 1959**

Raising our young family in the ministry environment was another daunting challenge. Of our three children, only Nevin seemed to adjust well to the urban setting. From a young age he cultivated two languages, the conventional English spoken by his Pennsylvania Dutch parents and the Ebonic "Chicagoese" of his playmates. We seldom had to worry about him; his friends, the neighborhood youth, would take care of him. Nina and Ann, on the other hand, from early ages struggled to adapt to West Side life.

After a few years spent in the Chicago public school system, Nina lagged considerably behind her grade level for academic abilities. While I tried to help the best I could, providing additional tutoring, homework help, and summer school, it became clear that the overcrowded, underresourced classroom wasn't doing her any good. Eventually we sent Nina and Ann with another West Side Christian Parish family to a private Catholic school on the South Side, where conditions were much more favorable. Yet the toll on Nina was beyond schooling. At a play school, Nevin and Nina were administered Rorschach tests, for which Nina described things associated with our blighted urban environment such as broken glass and rusted tin.

We had a hard time with Ann, who was often a sick baby. We took her to a doctor nearby, but he should have referred us much sooner to a specialist. So we went through all the antibiotics until they didn't do her any good anymore. She was throwing up every night. I was breastfeeding and she couldn't swallow, so I wiped her mouth. But I was wiping the milk that she should have been drinking. Later on I gave her supplements, which was basically all she was living on. She was seven pounds three ounces when she was born, and she was ten pounds at seven months. And she was always cheerful. Even when she threw up, we'd clean her off, clean the bed, and she smiled. I think that's why she's such a compassionate person now. It was humbling, that she was such a sick child. It became increasingly clear to me that our family wasn't doing well, and that we would have to find a way out of the West Side soon.

I found myself in conflict with what was expected of me and what I was able to give to our ministry. I was trying to be "all things to all people," available and capable on all fronts of our outreach, and unable to admit that ministry in that way might not have been for me. I didn't have a sense of who I really was. I thought that if you just showed these people what life can be like, that they'll want it. After all, who wouldn't? I wanted to do everything just right, which was impossible. That kind of attitude sets you up for burning out, which is what happened to me and Julius.

In our six years on Peoria Street, I would say that my relationship with Julius had us stuck in separate tracks, working alongside each other but not communicating or deeply sharing each other's experience. While Julius spent his days outside of the house pursuing his various community projects, I found myself in an uncomfortable environment, managing a struggling young family, isolated among neighbors I couldn't connect with, expected to fulfill a calling to be a model for radical Christian hospitality.

We didn't learn how to communicate as a family until after things broke down for us.

We didn't know what to do: one day Julius would want to leave and I wouldn't, and another day, it was the other way around. And where would we go? Reba was the natural place to go to because they knew us. They were being a model of the church, and I didn't quite understand that. But I didn't see that they were doing anything for the poor. We finally did decide to go for a sabbatical which turned out to be a move. I rode with David Gale in a truck with our stuff and I cried all the way.

We thought that three of the African-American matriarchs from Church of Hope would move up with us, but they washed out. We had stuff in place for one, Mattie May, to cook for the Reba nursery school. But when they thought about leaving their families, they couldn't quite make it.

Thinking back to our Church of Hope days, I'm not sure I'd have gone there if we had made a clear evaluation of what we were doing. But when you're young and you dream, you're not always realistic. A few of the things we did right was that I was a stay-at-home mother. I chose to have the washer and dryer in my house, which is why folks came through to do their laundry with us. It was good for them to come through and it made life interesting.

VII. Settling In at Reba Place Fellowship in Evanston

When we moved to Reba we did not think about making this our permanent home. The only thing we knew for sure was that we needed a place to start over, to set realistic expectations for ourselves, and to recollect as a family.

When we came, Louise Miller gave us little brown envelopes with our weekly grocery money, like each other family at Reba. So we had some sense of being conscious of money and how we live together. That was very important. But we weren't living in a poor situation anymore. I was beginning to get adjusted, and I certainly knew that we didn't want the whole world to be like Maxwell Street. Back on Peoria Street we had two trees on our block, a cottonwood and a mulberry. But in Evanston, we had all these trees and lots of grass all over the place. We felt much better that our children had that environment.

Early on, I asked John Miller, the founder of Reba Place, to promise that we would never become a Mennonite congregation. He knew better than to promise something that he had no control of. In Pennsylvania, in

Lancaster County, I thought the Mennonites were very cliquish, keeping mostly to themselves, a little self-righteous. But I had a good experience when Bethany Seminary partnered with the General Conference Mennonites. They had a busload come up from Woodlawn Avenue every day and we took our classes together, except for Mennonite history and Church of the Brethren history. That was a good experience. It's a wonder to me now how I came through that good experience and was still hanging back from being a Mennonite.

We came to Reba pretty broken down, starting at the bottom. John and Louise Miller met with us for counseling. Julius had a hard time finding a job when employers knew he was a trained pastor. They thought that if they gave him a job he'd pursue some kind of overt religious agenda or become unhappy and return to the ministry. It was about six weeks until he had a job, first with a youth employment agency, and then at a state mental hospital. Even when Julius was so busy, he bicycled down to the Main Evanston Library and would come home with twelve books, which was the maximum they allowed. Every noontime he read to our kids from the library books. They had an hour and fifteen minutes for lunch. Julius was very good about that. He was a little rushed on some other things, but not that.

We did a lot of waffling and doubting before we came, but when the kids were in Evanston and in school, we got rooted—at least I got rooted pretty fast. I didn't want to pick up and go any time soon. Our kids did have to catch up from their poor schools. But Nevin, he didn't have trouble anywhere. He had skipped a grade in Chicago. When he came to Evanston, they put him ahead. The girls had a harder time. Ann was very shy and very quiet. At school she wouldn't say anything. When the teacher complained to us, I talked with her. She told me, "They always say keep quiet, keep quiet, and I keep quiet!"

Nina had the hardest time with reading and math. She never caught on to reading until she and I worked with patterns for sewing a dress. After that she learned how to read recipes to cook. From then on she sewed most of her own clothes in Nichols Middle School. It was the hippy era, then. One day when children came out of school, I saw that everyone's jeans were shredded. Nina looked the best of them all in her own home-sewn clothes. Now she outdoes me at everything. She's versatile, I'll tell you. I still cook by a recipe. She can make something out of whatever she has there, and that blows my mind. So I laugh and say that whatever I did, she did better.

In that period our kids did well. They had so many peers and they were all in a youth group that was its own subculture. James Ewing and Ruth Anne were their leaders some of the time. They went to Koinonia Farm for a week or two; on that trip Nevin came back with all his underwear the color of clay from going to the swimming hole. They also went to Plow Creek in the very early days and cleaned the garbage out of their first house in the valley. The Fellowship fostered these activities very well. They had a very strong youth group that admonished Nevin when he flirted with some girls at Plow Creek: "That's not what we do!"

Tim Brown and Nevin took a Renault (a little French compact car) apart in the basement at Elmwood to redo it. They laid everything down on the floor in the order they took it off. Nevin wasn't old enough to drive yet, so they drove it in the alleys. When Nevin finished high school, he and Daniel Roddy went on a Mennonite Central Committee assignment in France. When Nevin left for that assignment, he said, "I can't understand why anybody would be a counselor—people are just too much, such a bother." He didn't have any feeling of commitment to Reba Place. So we didn't know what would happen. But somehow or other he started valuing what Reba was about, and when he came back he wanted to be a practicing member, and that was a joy to us.

Dorothy Day visited us back when we had been at Reba just six months. In the basement we had a coffeehouse with couches, tables, and musicians or speakers. She admitted that the Catholic Worker doesn't promote good family life and that some of the marriages in the community came apart when they were part of the Catholic Worker movement. She was pretty outspoken generally, but she wasn't rude. She saw that we gave a lot of energy to raising our families. I think we had some familiarity with what she would say. We had read her writings, like *Loaves and Fishes*, and we paid attention. We looked to her with a lot of admiration.

VIII. Extended Family Household Life at the Clearing

The Clearing Household at 722 Monroe got started when we were in a small group with Tom and Betty Roddy. Tom was on a rampage because of his bipolar condition. Julius and some of the others helped him get into the mental hospital. Betty said she really wished someone would come and help with her children. She had nine kids but two were gone already. It was pretty clear that Betty was overwhelmed. She was on this Catholic thing of having lots of babies, but she didn't like the mothering part. So Julius's mind got working, figuring out how it might work. I wasn't in favor of it at first. Nevin said, "No don't do it! Mom's style and Betty's style are very different. It won't work." I was leery; I just didn't know.

In some ways, I think we should have followed Nevin's advice. That was a very, very hard year. Judith Mendel had come from the Hutterites, from a full communal life, so we made sure she was moving in with us. Ann Hecht was there with her three-week-old baby; she was in a broken family situation and just couldn't handle it alone. We agreed to have her come. That baby would literally get awake if you dropped a pin on the floor. Some of the other people in the household weren't dependable or at peace with themselves. That was the mixture of people that we had. It was a very hard time.

At that time we learned about the Church of the Redeemer in Houston where they were doing large households. Hilda and Betty were sent to check them out. They came back all glowing about the miracles happening there. So Reba pretty much modeled ourselves off their pattern of extended households. We were the first large household at Reba. Soon after, pretty much everyone at Reba was living in large, extended-family households.

I didn't do very well that first year. There was just a lot of tension. I don't think Betty really wanted us to be here. It was a love/hate situation. I had never lived with anyone who changed moods in twenty minutes. And I wasn't the person that I thought that I would be either. I was bothered by that. Tom Roddy was back around and would not take his medication. We were with the Roddy family for about eighteen months. It was a bad idea. I just say the Lord was gracious to us, and we're all still on speaking terms now after some of the mistakes we've made.

We ate every meal together then. Nina and Mary, who were in middle school, made a meal together every week. They would make a jello salad after school one day, make a cake the next night, and then the next night they would make a main dish and serve the meal. They were taking a lot of responsibility and being very mature. But they didn't help to make decisions, and that was wrong. We didn't catch on to that right away and we didn't improve the situation. Mary wanted to join the Fellowship, and there was considerable discussion about it because that was a little early for making such a lifelong decision. Anne Stewart thought that Mary should be allowed to join and we didn't agree with that.

Eventually, Hilda was ready to take on Betty and her kids. Hilda had a much more expandable mind and wasn't ruffled if Betty wasn't finding a satisfying life situation. Nevin had Daniel Roddy for a friend, and Nina had Mary: there were lots of things that were good about it. And then Dave and Neta Jackson moved in. They were very creative. We played lots of games. And the relationships with other people in the household were quite good. We were goofy together: I remember a time when we had our hands on the person in front of us and we went up the steps and back down the steps singing the "Heffalumps and Woozles" song from *Winnie the Pooh*. The Jacksons were so good at that creativity, and those were some of the best years of our life.

IX. My Call to Hospitality on Behalf of the Fellowship

I was already doing hospitality for the community. In those days the Fellowship was famous and we had many visitors. Neta Jackson, Minna Regier, and I met every Monday morning with the letters from people who wanted to come. We sent them to the different households. Eventually we got guest apartments that we furnished nicely. Soon I did most of the hospitality work myself. When most of the households dissolved around 1980, then I arranged for visitors to sleep in the guest apartment and have meals at different homes. I would wash the sheets and the towels, make the beds and replenish the breakfast food. I did that plus all the phoning arrangements. I don't know how I did it. I filled that role for over forty years until 2012 when my hearing loss made communicating with would-be guests too difficult to do over the phone. It never got boring because the people were always different. I really didn't tire of all that. My parents hosted a lot of guests. I guess that carried over from my growing up.

X. Reflections on Extended Family Household Living

At first we had to transition from being a family of five with our own children to joining another family, so we had to tone down some of our own traditions. Eventually we grew to eleven and then eighteen people. This caused our children to feel like they were being left out. We expected our children to take responsibilities like an adult, but they did not have a vote when decisions were made. That wasn't fair. I regret that, but we're very blessed that we've been able to talk these things over and be reconciled.

Our household sometimes went on vacations together. One time we went to Upstate New York and accidentally left Nina behind at a gas station. At the next stop, an hour later, we got ice cream cones and realized there was one extra cone and no Nina. We went back. The man at the service station thought we were trying to get rid of her. Nina was thirteen or fourteen at the time.

With that many people living together, at some point you blow it. Then you talk it over, pick up the pieces and start again. By living in a large household you find out things about yourself you'd rather not know. Maybe we get wiser.

**Peggy in the Clearing household photo: 2014,
with Julius to her right and Hilda Carper on her left**

I always say that community is a very delicate thing. It just takes one person going haywire in leadership to form a schism, and it all comes crashing down. We've had our hard relationships, but our attitude was that it's more important that we are kept together in the bond of love than to follow this particular issue or belief. That's a big thing for us. Another thing that might be a good lesson is that consensus decision-making helps bring people on board. I really appreciate it. We did strict consensus for a long time. That's a little cumbersome. Now, if you try to have consensus and it doesn't come along, the proposal goes ahead if it has an 85 percent majority vote.

XI. Reflections on Racial Reconciliation Efforts at Reba

Our community continues to reach out across racial and ethnic barriers, but segregation is still a problem. We have had some very positive relationships with people of different races. Following the Civil Rights era, Vincent Harding and his wife, Rose Marie, lived with us for a year as they recovered from burnout. More recently, I would go shopping with our neighbor, Martha McDonald. Julius has made many friends in the neighborhood by caring for them in times of crisis. The Fellowship has had people of color as members, mostly women and adopted children. But we're still a pretty racially homogenous bunch. The bond we have as a community makes it hard for people of other races to break in. If we were smaller or more scattered, maybe like the Reba colony living in Rogers Park where our daughter Nina and Ronn Frantz live with Nieta Jones, we'd have a better and more accessible experience. But negotiating all the different languages and cultures there is exhausting. Hilda Carper thinks that's what heaven will be like. I just hope I have the capacity to receive it all!

XII. On Family and Community Life

We have learned to take time for both family and household. Now Nina and I talk every Wednesday morning. Sometimes we work on sewing projects. Julius and Nevin meet each week too. Julius and I would take time out every Tuesday, go out to eat, catch up. It's just for us. We also do errands together. That cuts down on arguments. My parents didn't have their arguments in front of us kids. But Julius and I are free to disagree in front of the household. They know we love each other. It's okay.

Present and Accessible

David Hovde

In late 1993, when I was twenty-three years old, living with my parents in central Illinois, and lacking a sense of direction for my life, I arranged a visit to learn more about Reba, and to test the possibility of participating in the community life. When I arrived at 722 Monroe Street in Evanston (a.k.a. "The Clearing Household"), Peggy Belser, Reba's hospitality coordinator, was there to greet me.

"Hovde—that's a Mennonite name," Peggy observed. I explained that my parents were not "ethnic Mennonites" but had joined a Mennonite church when I was young. I did not know any other Hovdes who were Mennonites. Peggy said that she had corresponded with a Mennonite, Linda Hovde, downstate. I told her that Linda was my mother. Peggy seemed genuinely excited to meet me and make the connection. It turns out that Peggy kept track of many people, and seldom forgot a name.

During that visit, I learned that folks at the Clearing ate nearly all their meals together, an important ritual to them. They let the phone ring during mealtimes, refusing to interrupt their conversation. At that time in my life, I felt very lonely and was attracted to the idea of a household "family" that valued mealtimes together.

Sometime after that visit, back home in Normal, Illinois, I decided I wanted to move to Reba, but lacked the courage to call Peggy and let her know. Finally, at 12:00 noon, I worked up the courage to make the call. During the conversation, Peggy seemed to readily accept my wish to move to Reba ASAP, without having any job prospects there. However, she seemed irritated that I had called at noon, since I knew they were ready to sit down to lunch. I hurriedly ended the conversation and hung up. I was learning that Peggy has a wonderful gift of hospitality and welcome, but also guards the boundaries that she and the household need for a wholesome life.

Peggy's gift of hospitality is legendary at Reba and beyond. Over the years, when guests came, Peggy greeted them and entered into relaxed, friendly conversation with them. She would remember details about the guests. For example, Peggy remembers what Henri Nouwen wore when he visited decades ago (a V-neck sweater and corduroy pants).

Two words sum up who Peggy is for me—*present* and *accessible*. When she is not doing household work, talking on the phone to potential guests, or doing some other project, she often sits in the living room to read, pray, or do word puzzles, ready to visit with anyone who comes by. Unlike Julius, who would often serve others by meeting in his office to work on their problems, Peggy would serve others in a more relaxed way by being present and available to them.

At the Clearing I learned to take my turn as a cook. I would often ask Peggy for advice about putting on a meal. I don't remember a time when she responded in a way that communicated "Don't talk to me!"

In my early years at the Clearing, when Peggy made the grocery lists, did the shopping, or coordinated the many details of household life, she would regularly give me unsolicited advice about cooking or housekeeping, sometimes in a teasing way. I would react resentfully by saying nothing, or by expressing my differing opinions defensively. One time when I was washing my clothes, she told me with a grin, "I've never seen a load like that before," referring to my oversized basket of laundry. Gradually, over time, I learned to leave aside my defensiveness and share my opinions in a more straightforward way like Peggy, trusting in her love for me.

Over the years, at the Clearing, Peggy's husband, Julius, was the "Head of Household," Peggy was the "Household Manager," and Hilda Carper (their longtime friend and housemate) was the "Assistant Household Manager." These three were in ministry together already in the late 1950s and early 1960s in inner-city Chicago. Hilda joined them again around 1980. Julius at the Clearing, Peggy, and Hilda then teamed up to lead the household for three decades, before handing over the leadership to younger household members, with their blessing.

Julius was always the compassionate one who would urge people to be more welcoming to those in need. He would say that the Clearing table could seat eighteen people. This would evoke an exasperated "Julius!" from Peggy. (The rest of us thought fifteen was a more realistic number.) Peggy and Hilda used to tease Julius and say that his favorite song should be "Fill My House unto the Fullest."

Julius would welcome homeless people into the Clearing, give them something to eat, and then leave them for Peggy and Hilda to relate to while he went downstairs to his office for another meeting. It seemed to Peggy and Hilda that the Clearing could not function well if Julius welcomed in every homeless person that came by, so they brainstormed with other Evanston church and city leaders how to start a homeless shelter. Hilda became its first director, and when she retired, the shelter was named "Hilda's Place."

Peggy observes that Julius and Hilda were both leaders who liked to lead. Peggy, however, is happy doing what needs to be done, but does not like giving others directions. She says that Hilda did not hesitate to give others directions, and neither did Julius, once he decided it was necessary. Peggy, on the other hand, has a quiet wisdom that others respect, and is grounded in her values, so she can make clear decisions and not waver on them. The gifts of the Spirit flow from her hands and words. She teaches us how to be confident in God's love, and she shares that love freely with everyone around her.

I want to end by sharing about Peggy's relationship with a housemate who could be cold, and would mostly keep to himself. When Peggy was in the living room, she'd ask him for help with her word puzzles, and he would pitch in. Her calm, peaceful spirit would help him relax and open up to her like with no one else in the house. I greatly appreciate that gift of Peggy's.

David Hovde has lived at the Clearing for twenty years now and is one of the present members of the household's leadership team. He works as a caregiver for a housemate, is Reba Place Fellowship's current hospitality coordinator following Peggy, and is also a member of Reba Place Fellowship's leadership team. He is grateful to Peggy, Julius, and Hilda for welcoming him into their lives and for modeling for him how to live out the way of Christ.

A Kitchen and Living Room Kind of Ministry

Carol Steiner

I arrived at Reba in August of 1965. That first week I had a meal in every family's home. I remember going to the Belsers's on the second floor at 714 Reba Place where the house had a third-floor turret with a round space beneath it. There were benches around three sides of a kitchen table that jutted out into the room so more chairs could be added. I'd never seen homemade furniture like that, so obviously designed for hospitality.

Julius and Peggy were alike in that they both knew how to improvise whatever space and whatever stuff they had to make it work for hospitality. Julius would invite people, Peggy would fill in. They had the same mission, compassion, and style. Julius would listen to people in his office in a pastoral kind of way and pray with them. With Peggy it might be a cup of tea, a stool under your feet, relaxed comfort, a listening ear, and a tissue box nearby in case someone had to cry. She had the same pastoral ministry as Julius, only in a kitchen and living room kind of way.

One dear memory I have of Peggy is how she made a wedding cake for Albert and me. Peggy didn't want guests to feel "second class" because they only got a piece of plain sheet cake. Peggy made little layer cakes decorated with gold leaves for every table, in the same style as the big cake that Albert and I cut to feed each other.

Back when Albert and I were newly married, women used to iron all the clothes. (Now with perma-press cloth no one does that anymore.) I remember lugging my laundry basket, my iron, and the ironing board over to Peggy's house so we could iron together, and talk. If I called Peggy to ask, "Can I come over?" her answer was always "Yes." As a new homemaker, she taught me how to turn ordinary household chores into a lot of fun. She became like a second mother to me.

In those days Julius and Peggy maintained connections with the people they had lived with on Peoria Street, on Chicago's West Side. So, the Belsers, Albert, and I would go visit them in their apartments. This was my first contact with the extreme poverty of Black folks who could not escape the ghetto. I was surprised by how warmly we were welcomed. Julius, Peggy, and Albert knew how to be with them, so I could follow along.

Sometimes we were invited for birthday celebrations. One African-American woman was diabetic, so Peggy knew better than to bake her an ordinary birthday cake. Instead, with her usual creativity, she bought a big round piece of cheese the size of a cake and decorated it with cream cheese as frosting. It looked like the real thing. The "cheese cake" perfectly fit her friend's diet and gave a big boost to her food budget.

In my early years at Reba Place Fellowship, Peggy, other women, and I would prepare a meal for Fellowship work days. No one needed to be in charge. Peggy would see what food was on hand and start in. It always worked out. And at our evening meetings, which often ran long, Peggy had a knack for saying something surprising that would cut through the tension and make us all laugh. She seemed to be made by God for community.

Many years ago, when Peggy found out I was going to have back surgery, she offered to go grocery shopping with me to help carry the bags. It never would have occurred to me to ask for this kind of help. After my back healed, we continued shopping together for decades until Albert retired and could help me do it. Because of my severe environmental allergies, I often had to wear a mask when I went out, and I had to shop at Whole Foods to get organic produce. Many times, in the produce section we'd get to talking about our childhood memories. Once Peggy saw a big mushroom and told me how her sister made those into vegetarian sandwiches. Little pickles would set Peggy talking about how her mom grew and canned pickles like that. However late we got home, it didn't matter. A tight companionship grew up between us. In our kitchens our phones had long cords so we could work for hours and keep talking.

Later, when my allergies got so severe that I couldn't go to Fellowship meetings, Peggy would come over every Wednesday afternoon and fill me in on community events. She had a phenomenal memory that didn't miss a thing.

Peggy was smart in her own way. She completed a seminary degree in religious education at the same time as Julius. Except for keeping house, working half-time at the local hospital switch board to earn money, and birthing a baby, she "didn't have anything else to do, so why not?"

Peggy is totally generous and genuine. If I needed help with a quilt, she'd drop off her whole box of threads so I could find what matched. There was a constant exchange of supplies between us. And Peggy could receive as easily as give. Peggy made matching shirts for Julius and Nevin just before the whole family set out on a bicycle vacation trip. That was striking and impressed me. We shared similar exasperations about our husbands with lots of humor and mutual encouragement to hang in there.

Peggy graciously extended her living room across the street into our house because I was housebound much of the time. She was observant about what it takes to make a healthy living space for me. For example, I couldn't go into a room for half an hour after it was cleaned. But Peggy "got it"; she understood what I needed.

For fifty-four years we've been hanging out together like this with never a fight, never "on the outs" with each other. We might have differences of opinion, but never an argument. Peggy's capacity for relationships and her ability to find some point of connection with everyone is phenomenal. She is the soul of community in a way that draws no attention to herself.

Last December (2018), Julius's life with Peggy ended. Since then, Peggy modeled grief for me too. I saw Peggy standing at the casket, smoothing down Julius's coat and tie. She said through her tears, "That isn't him. It's just a shell." Later, she would share with me how she experienced Julius's last moments. Like their many years together, this was a family time, house full of children, their spouses, grandchildren and great-grandchildren. Julius's siblings were also part of the family. Peggy told me about their visits in great detail. Then one day she showed me all the sympathy cards she had received and said she was ready to put them away. She wanted to move on with her life in the household and Fellowship. She is back to reading books (one every two days) and assembling jigsaw puzzles (one every day) while visiting with guests and friends. She is open about missing Julius, and yet she is free to move on with making a life for herself.

I wonder, how did someone like Peggy happen? She grew up in a family furniture store where she was continually meeting new people. Her parents always had guests at the Sunday table. She grew up in a home where her mother shared goods freely and her father made loans to customers without a piece of paper, or even a handshake. She grew up with excellent role models. But she didn't just inherit good habits. She and Julius spent many hours talking over their experiences with different kinds of people. That is how they maintained such a close unity of mission and spirit. Peggy has learned to live in the present, to let go of judgmental thoughts, to solve problems with what is given, and to welcome people as they come. She doesn't talk a lot about her faith, she just does it.

∼

Carol (Huddleston) married Albert Steiner in 1965 and with him raised their daughter, Karen. Carol has served Reba Place Fellowship as bookkeeper, as an outside earner in secretarial work, and as a mentor for RPF interns. As she has been more confined by environmental illness, Carol is widely appreciated as a faithful intercessor and anchor in the church's prayer chain.

THREE

Hilda Carper

Loyal Truth-Teller, Artist of Community, Sister to the Least

I. EARLY LIFE AND FAMILY

I was born March 4, 1927, in an unheated bedroom of an old farmhouse in Lancaster County, Pennsylvania. Before the doctor came, I arrived with the cord around my neck. Otherwise, who knows, I could have been a genius!

I was the third of four children. The first three of us—Ruth, then Jimmy, and then me—each arrived sixteen months apart; then sister Jean tagged along four years later. We lived on an isolated farm, which was pretty primitive by today's standards; we didn't have running water or electricity until I was about twelve.

My mother was a school teacher. Along with being a housewife and mother, she would sometimes take substitute teaching jobs in the little one-room schools that dotted our landscape. My father, growing up on a Mennonite farm, never went further than eighth grade. As a result, there was this disparity between his education and interests and my mother's, and that exacerbated his belief that he must be "head" of his wife and family to legitimate his sense of self-worth. Our dad was a difficult man to live with. Today, he would likely be diagnosed with bipolar disorder. The tenor of our family tended to go up and down with his changing moods. Not knowing how to understand his low swings, he would blame them on our mother and punish her by not speaking to her (except to scold), often for weeks at a time. When he had a spat with someone outside the family, our mother would have a reprieve from his anger, and we kids were greatly relieved.

My brother Jim, unfortunately, was disaffected from the church and spent most of his life as a scoffer in relation to spiritual things. We loved him no matter what, but it was difficult. His cynical spirit may be due, in part, to our father, who never seemed able to bond with my brother and was often quite cruel to him.

Mother was the center of our family and was very idealistic. It was really hard for her to see who the man she had married was becoming and how it affected our family. She tried constantly to please him and build him up in our eyes, to point out all the good things she could find in him. But we didn't buy it. She was also a teacher at heart and directed our intellectual life carefully. She made sure we had good books to read, and nature guides, so we could identify the birds and butterflies, plants and rocks. She would spend hours reading to us what they today call "chapter books." She made sure we didn't read those pseudo-Christian novels that she felt were more froth than faith.

These were the days of the Great Depression. We always had enough to eat because we were on a farm, but like most people living through this period, we were very poor. For extra money, my mother would write articles for a farm magazine called *The Rural New Yorker*. Her column was "Garden Spot Notes," since Lancaster County was called the Garden Spot. She was an early soybean advocate and shared some good recipes using them. At the same time, she had to be a farmer's wife, working in the fields and helping with the livestock. At night when everyone else was in bed was when she would do the things she enjoyed: writing and reading. She would quote poetry to us, bits that fit situations as they emerged.

I remember my least favorite thing about the farm was picking strawberries because this hurt my legs. I also hated the smell of fresh asparagus, which I had to help bundle for the market. We girls were never required to work on the farm. When it was time to harvest the strawberries and other market crops, we used hired help. My mother would often have to supervise these workers. We kids sometimes worked with them, too, and got paid, though not as much as the grown-ups.

Our farm was fairly small, with a couple of cows, some pigs, and horses. It was what is called a "truck farm," meaning that we raised a variety of produce that we trucked to market. Sometimes we contracted with companies like Campbell's to harvest a whole bunch of tomatoes.

We lived on three different farms during my first twelve years. During the Depression, my father failed to make it on his own with the first farm, so after that we farmed other people's land.

That I grew up in the Mennonite Church was the most significant influence in forming my spirituality. In those days, our type of Mennonites lived more separate from "the world." My sense of the church, from early on, was that we were a "special" people separate from the world. It might be similar to the Jewish sense of peoplehood—not against the world, but special in relation to the world. The Mennonite garb set us apart from "the world" especially when we went to town and to school. This gave me a very deep sense of identity, which I think is rather rare, at least in the Western White world. Like the Jews, African Americans, Amish, and other minority cultural groups, this peoplehood includes an awareness of a long history that my ancestors were a part of, that long Anabaptist tradition. This was at least true of my mother's side of the family. We weren't sure about my father's lineage. There are very few Carpers among Mennonites, but it is a common Jewish surname.

When I was about fourteen, we moved out of Lancaster County to a small Mennonite colony in southeastern Virginia. This was in 1942, during World War II. The colony was an even smaller Mennonite context than what I'd come from in Pennsylvania. As I look back on it, it seems to me now like the intentional communities of today. The community was probably about two or three square miles of farms on what had been a large, historic plantation. In the early 1900s, people were recruited to colonize it. Word spread out to Mennonites in Ohio and Pennsylvania, and some came to settle it—sort of like homesteading. There were a few non-Mennonites settled within that area as well, but it became known then, as it still is, as "the Mennonite Colony." By the time our family moved there, it was a well-developed community. The fun thing for us teenagers was that we didn't feel isolated anymore; everyone lived close together and there was a large and wonderfully vibrant youth group. That was delightful for my siblings and me, since we hadn't known anything like that in Lancaster County.

I was baptized at the age of twelve, back when we were still in Lancaster County. That was the beginning of a more intensive spiritual life for me, but it wasn't the result of it. At first I was motivated by the fear that if I didn't get baptized and "join the church" before I died, then I would go to hell, so I thought, "I had better get that taken care of." Baptism, along with difficulties with my parents' marriage, did, however, begin a very personal relationship for me with the Lord. During my teenage years, I had a very intensive spiritual life. It was not connected with Bible studies or Sunday school or youth group discussions, because we didn't have much of that. In the milieu of my day, people didn't talk about their personal spiritual experiences, and so my early life with the Lord was a very private affair. During that time I memorized lots of Scripture. From stories I'd read about missionaries and persecution, I imagined that someday I might be imprisoned for my faith, and if that happened to me without a Bible, I wanted to have the Scriptures in my head. This was the beginning, for me, of a lifelong fascination with the Bible. I learned that in order to memorize verses, I had to think deeply about what they meant. Most of my lifelong intensive Scripture study has been a personal endeavor rather than corporate or academic study.

II. College and Abroad

Hilda as a high school graduate

I graduated from high school at seventeen and went to what is now Eastern Mennonite University for a year. After that I taught for a year in the parochial school started by my mother in our home church. Then I went to Goshen College, taking off a year to work with children's groups in the Detroit Mennonite Mission. I finally graduated from Goshen in 1950. Then I taught first and second grade school in Fisher, Illinois (near Champaign).

After that I decided to serve with the Mennonite Central Committee, our denominational relief and service agency. I hoped to do a two-year term in some distant place like China, but Orie Miller, who interviewed me, informed me that the only assignments available were five years either as a teacher in Africa or taking over the children's church curriculum project that my sister Ruth was soon to leave in Basel, Switzerland. "Furthermore," he said forcefully, "you shouldn't be thinking about getting married during that time." That raised a huge cry among my friends. They would say things like, "After all, you'll be twenty-nine when your term ends. These are the years you *should* be thinking about getting married. DON'T DO IT!" I was given two weeks to make my decision. How could I decide such a weighty matter in such a short time?

This resulted in one of those seminal religious experiences one has now and again in the course of their life. I thought hard about the possible lifelong implications of the decision. I also had a premonition that if I let God in on it, I would be headed to Basel to write curriculums, which would definitely not be an exotic adventure. Since my teen years I had lived around our dining room table strewn with the curriculums my mother was working on for our denomination. Besides that, I had my sister's letters from Basel, which didn't exactly amount to "exotic adventures." But somewhere between Goshen, Indiana (where I'd had my interview), and my destination of Champaign, Illinois, I said to God, "OK now, I'm ready to take the risk. I'll open my mind so you can tell me which way to take: stay at home and get married (hopefully), or teach in Africa, or sit at a desk and write curriculum in Basel."

Still expecting that God would need at least two weeks to come up with an answer for me, I settled back in my seat to listen. Almost immediately, the answer was there, "Basel," and also a deep settled sense that it was a *good* choice. Instead of dread came joy and excitement in the prospect. It felt like a miracle to me. In the years that followed, which were not fun and games, I never had to second-guess my decision. I knew it was God-given, and that was all that mattered.

I was in Europe from January 1953 to June 1957. My time there transformed how I interacted with the Bible. My assignment was editing and writing Bible lessons for children that were translated into German and French; they were for use in Mennonite and other European free churches. This required having gutsy encounters with the Scriptures. In order to make them accessible for children, I had to distill the text for myself. An elderly man named Cornelius Wall, with a doctorate in biblical studies from Princeton, oversaw our work. Like many other Mennonite families, they had fled from Russia during the Soviet Revolution. The Walls were able to escape through Turkey, but their infant daughter died of starvation along the way. "Onkel Wall" became an important biblical and spiritual mentor for me during those years.

There were three of us women on staff: German, French, and American, who shaped and guided the project. I would write in English and could edit in German, but not in French. We became close, lifelong friends. We lived together with other MCC workers in a household, where we spoke French, German, Swiss German, and English. We could all speak at least two of these languages, but none of us could communicate in all of them. Still, we managed, translating for each other as necessary.

When I first went to Switzerland, I worked for several months with my sister Ruth until her term ended. My younger sister, Jean, and her husband, Bob Miller (son of Orie Miller), came through Basel to visit me on their way home from an MCC term in Indonesia. In the five years that I was there, I saw no other family members, though there were lots of letters back and forth.

III. Back Home to the U.S.A.

In June 1957, when my term finished, I returned to my parents' home in Virginia, where once again I taught with my mother in the Mennonite elementary school for a year. The following fall I took a job at the MCC home office in Akron, Pennsylvania, for about a year. During that time, John Miller wrote to ask if I might want to join in their fledgling community in Evanston, Illinois. John and his wife, Louise, and I had been part of a "dreamers' group" in Basel made up of American Mennonite university students and MCC workers. We would sit around in our MCC house and talk about how to reform the Mennonite Church via intentional community. Since that time the Millers had gone to Goshen College, where John taught Bible and gathered some of the students who were interested in his ideas for Christian community. John and Louise, with some of their group, had "taken the plunge" in 1957 to create Reba Place Fellowship.

I decided to accept the invitation after meeting with them in January of 1959 at Julius and Peggy Belser's home in Chicago. And there it was decided I would spend that summer volunteering at the Church of Hope, the Belsers's inner-city community on Peoria Street, before settling in at Reba in the fall. After the summer, it seemed to me, and the others at Church of Hope and Reba Place, that I should stay and continue my work with the Belsers. They were establishing an intentional community in our little congregation there. It included African-American members from the neighborhood and us White "imports": Albert Steiner, Allan Howe, Jeanne Casner (later Howe), David and Margaret Gale, myself, and of course, the Belsers. The first and second year I taught in the public schools to earn my living, after which I came on staff in the West Side Christian Parish as Julius's pastoral assistant.

At the time, I also wrote curriculum for our purposes in the parish. I worked with Rosemary Barth, wife of University of Chicago professor, Markus Barth. Rosemary was also writing curriculum for her Baptist church in South Chicago. So we got together and traded ideas quite a bit. I also spent many weekends of "R & R" in their peaceful home in Hyde Park.

Down on Peoria street, I directed a children's choir, all made up of neighborhood kids. We became a very good little choir that was invited to sing in many suburban churches around Chicago. A couple of times we were invited to sing on TV, including once for a popular clown program that invited us to sing at their televised Christmas bash at a real circus in Medina Temple in Chicago. We sang with a lion in a cage right next to us!

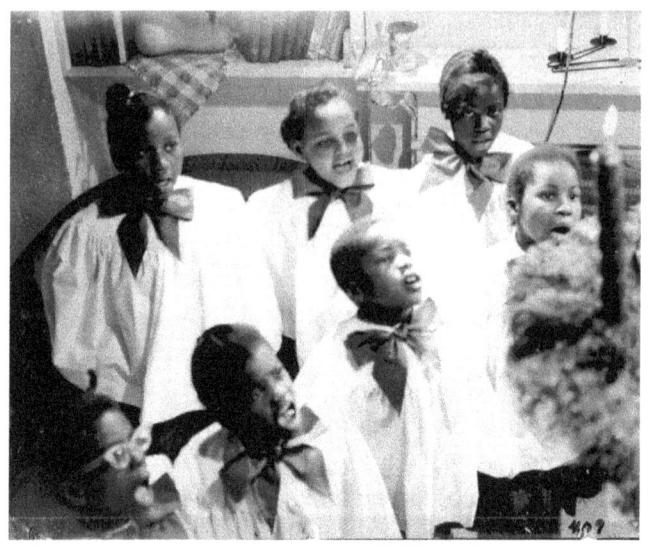

Hilda's children's choir under an Advent wreath

Hilda sorting choir robes

Music had always been a love of mine. Wherever I was, I made sure I connected with a good choir that I could sing with. When I first came to Chicago, I sang for ten years with the Chicago Symphony Chorus, under Margaret Hillis, a nationally known choral conductor. Eventually I left when I felt that God wanted me to serve the kingdom in other ways, though my parents always felt I could have been a professional musician.

During these Peoria Street days, I became engaged to a young Methodist minister who served in a small church in the Pilsen area of Chicago. Falling in love deeply enough to start planning a life together brought out a side of me that I hadn't seen since childhood. I loved the prospect of having someone to take care of me. Unfortunately, I didn't take this life-changing decision to the Lord, instead trusting friends for this discernment. It was my fiancé who realized that we were not meant for each other. He had become disenchanted with Christianity, and I was now "too religious" for him. I was devastated. But it occasioned for me a profound soul searching and an important time of learning to know myself more deeply. Eventually I realized that the Lord had rescued me from a disastrous path.

In 1965, urban renewal slated our area to be demolished to make room for the University of Illinois's Circle Campus. Our little church on Peoria Street was coming to an end. We hoped to stay together and explored a number of possibilities in Chicago, but none of them seemed right. So we explored moving to Reba Place. For six months we all came to Reba Place for Sunday morning worship. Everyone, including our African-American members, enjoyed the services and the Reba folks. Still, the suburbs and Reba Place were foreign to them, and in the end, they settled for the familiar, as did we middle-class White members. The African Americans scattered to various inner-city locations, and the rest of us came to Reba.

IV. Ministry at Reba

I moved to Reba in June of 1966, just before the civil rights uprisings in Chicago, when some buildings in our Peoria Street neighborhood were set on fire. In Evanston, I lived at 727 Reba Place, on the third floor. Immediately after moving to Reba I spent the summer preparing the first floor of 727 for a daycare center I was asked to set up and lead. It wasn't intended for Reba children, although some Reba kids did come to it. At first, I did everything from the cooking to cleanup. I liked that; it felt like making a home for these kids. As more children came there were more administrative tasks like preparing reports for the city and the state. Eventually enrollment at Reba Daycare Center grew to where we needed helpers, so we hired a cook and preschool teachers. As my administrative role grew, I no longer felt like I was making a little nest for kids; it was more like a regular school. When the Fellowship asked me to stop and come to work on more pastoral and leadership functions for the community, I wasn't sad to leave the daycare because I wasn't as interested in what I was doing there anymore.

My friend Catherine Wirth, from Germany, was only fourteen years old when I first met her in Switzerland. Years later she came to the United States through the Mennonite Exchange program. Shortly after I moved to Reba, she came to visit, to see if Reba might be the place for her. She's been here ever since!

John and Joanna Lehman, who had lived with us for several years at 727 Reba, moved out, and we became a household of single people. In 1967, this was the first household, several years before there were other established households. The women lived on the second and third floors. The first floor was the nursery school. Most of the single men lived on the third floor of Virgil and Joan Vogt's house at 726 Monroe Street across the alley. We singles would get together for dinner and take turns cooking. We went on tenting vacations together. Orwin Youngquist, Catherine Wirth, and Ruth Anne Friesen were all part of that scene, about a dozen of us total.

I moved again when Reba began its "household era," when nearly everyone was living in extended-family settings. We began the household at 714 Monroe with Jeanne and Allan Howe, Orwin, and a bunch of other younger folks.

Hilda visits a weary Dorothy Day at the Catholic Worker Farm in Tivoli, NY, 1970s

During that time, I was still teaching at the nursery school. The nursery school had grown and moved out of 727 Reba to the larger building where it is now, on the corner of Madison and Custer. I worked there until about 1976, when I began working for the church full time. Later on I was asked to lead a household at 720 Reba Place, where "The Patch" is now. When we became too many for 720, we all moved to 727 Reba, back to my first Reba home. Anne Stewart and Betty Roddy, with two girls and four boys between them, made it a very lively household! Bill and Maryanne Berry and their three young children, along with several other single folks, brought us to about eighteen in all.

What happened in the household was the leader's responsibility. When people didn't get along the leader had to become a mediator, and when people didn't get along with the leader, they had to find someone from outside the household to mediate. Along with the regimen of daily chores and tasks was the responsibility of being the contact person with the community leadership. I was also tapped for small group leadership and various other things. That was a period when the Fellowship was focused on its inner development with a lot of care for adults, rather than children. Despite the difficulties and lacks, it was a rich time.

Eventually, after several years of heading a large household, I was just burned out and wanted someone else to take over. I was beefing about this with the leadership for a year or so before the 727 household disbanded and I was finally released to live at the Clearing where Bob Lembke and I arrived on the same day. No one can remember exactly what year that was—sometime in the early eighties probably.

Another contribution that I made from the start when I came to Reba was helping in the development of worship life in the community. I had also done that sort of thing in our Peoria Street community. We put together the Hosanna songbook in those days. I collected the songs and hand-notated and lettered them, while Phyllis Schoewe did the tedious job of applying for permissions. One of my favorite parts was adapting musical pieces that I learned in Europe for our use with English lyrics.

From the very beginning, Reba was producing dramas in our community worship, something John Miller started. We used to have plays just about every Sunday, so in our archives are hundreds of plays that we don't use anymore, and I am sad for that. We didn't try to do anything fancy. We had a series of Old Testament, New Testament, and church history plays. A variety of people wrote them. We had a drama group and director who rehearsed the actors every Saturday or early Sunday morning. Also in those days, many original Reba worship songs were composed. It was a very fertile, creative time. Somebody would compose a song and bring it to the music group. We would arrange it with instruments and bring it to the congregation.

In addition to the other things I was involved in, I was also an elder, though the eldership was structured very differently than leadership is now. In the seventies we had three senior elders, each with four elders reporting to them. I certainly had more energy then than I do now. But I also have had problems in the past with doing perhaps too many things—which usually catches up with me.

In the early eighties, a seminary student and the pastor of Lake Street Church decided that Evanston needed a homeless shelter, but the city officials insisted that there would not be one. The congregation at Lake Street Church had quite a conflict with the city until a shelter was formed in their church basement. Peggy Belser and I went to volunteer because we had lots of homeless people coming to the Clearing, folks who had heard of us on Howard Street. Julius was very hospitable; he never turned any away, so it fell to Peggy and me to host them. Peggy and I wanted to find a way to support the homeless in a more stable way, so we started the breakfast program at the shelter. The ministry grew quickly, but the leadership of the shelter wasn't well organized to keep up with the growth. So after about six months, I was asked to be the director. I agreed to deal with everything except the finances, which would be left to others. When I eventually resigned (after about a decade), the shelter board decided to honor me by calling it "Hilda's Place," because the people on the street had always called it that.

Hilda with her mother, Eva Carper, who was cared for in the last years of her life at the Clearing household

My job included hiring (and firing) staff, recruiting and coordinating volunteers, and adding needed services. We set up a small clinic with volunteer doctors and nurses who were available to treat people at certain times in the week. We had only thirty beds at the time. Since then it's changed quite a bit, and they have added more programs in addition to the shelter. I did a lot of the administrative work from my home at the Clearing, which gave me some flexible time. Every night I had to be at the shelter before supper, and sometimes I didn't get back until 11:00 p.m., midnight, or even 2:00 in the morning, and then came home only to go back for breakfast a few hours later. It was a very life-giving job for me—like heading a household and running the nursery. The shelter was another opportunity for nest-making, for creating a nice place for people to live together.

After about ten years, I left the shelter with the prospect of working with some former Reba members in Spain, reaching out to form a healing community with ex-addicts. The ministry was going to expand to the U.S., and our friends in Spain were hoping I could work with the expansion. My dream was to head a little household out in the country somewhere, connected to the ministry organization and a local church. Then the head of the program suddenly stopped everything and said, "Oh no, a woman could never do that." I had already retired from the shelter in expectation of relocating to do this work, and suddenly I had neither job. It somehow felt right, though. I'm a start-up kind of person more than a developer who spreads out and organizes new programs.

After that turn of events, I was free to concentrate more on things within Reba Place Church. By that time the congregational sector was established separate from the Fellowship, and I was helping with both. I also continued working in pastoral leadership roles, mostly organizing worship and liturgy.

In 1997, I came down with an autoimmune disease, polymyalgia rheumatica. The attack was very sudden, and it took a while to be diagnosed. Since then I have had it chronically and have gotten progressively weaker. I handle it better than most with the help of steroids like Prednisone, but there have been lots of detrimental side effects to get used to. As I look at it now, things seemed to have happened providentially to me. I was able to make space in my life so that I didn't have to leave a job, only adjust the amount of work that I was doing each day.

Early in Reba's history there were people who longed to be in the countryside. At some point this desire was taken seriously, and folks began looking for available and affordable property in the rural areas outside of Chicago. At that point we weren't sure how it would play out. Would it be a new community or a retreat center? Would it become a source of produce? We looked at quite a number of farms that were for sale. Finally we found a place about two and a half hours west. An elderly recluse owned the farm and lived on it in a very haphazard fashion; you could say it was ill-kept. He raised pigs and let them run loose and burrow anywhere they pleased. He didn't have a proper plumbing system in the house, and there were tons of abandoned cars and car parts scattered around. The farm had only this one house on it that the owner had lived in. When he died the place had to be sold, so the Fellowship bought it. We cleaned and fixed it up enough so that the first Reba family to move there would have a halfway decent place to live.

The property did have a lot of potential—wonderful rolling hills, a beautiful forest, and large open fields. It was exciting to think how it could be developed. One family went down there with a group of teenagers led by Ruth Anne Friesen for a summer and helped clean up the place. Other Reba folk would come down to help for the weekends. It was an all-Fellowship project. Family by family, more people moved in as they built more housing.

Soon after its creation, it was decided that Plow Creek Fellowship, as it was eventually called, was to become its own community separate from Reba Place Fellowship. The farm evolved to raise produce for sale in the surrounding area with U-Pick kinds of crops, though they also ran their own sale barn and sold at farmers markets. At one point, I had some inheritance funds that helped Plow Creek build a retreat cabin not far away from their main campus, a place in the woods where you didn't have to see anyone else. I went there for a monthly retreat for a number of years. I would carry my water down and have kerosene lamps for light. I enjoyed it because it reminded me so much of my childhood. The cabin is still there and used by others for personal retreats.

V. Growing Old and Looking Back

Recently I was sitting on the porch of the Clearing looking out on Monroe Street and saw a number of us old-timers out and about. I just had to laugh because there were Julius and Peggy coming slowly down the street, holding on to each other. There was Albert with his cane, Vera with her walker, soon to be joined by me with my walker. I remember when all of us were hurrying down the streets bent on "important" business. We would joke about one day becoming old and sitting on our porches together.

That being said, it is a wonderful place to grow old. I am surrounded by all different ages, from babies up to other seniors. The Fellowship is a place that cares for, honors, and makes a useful space for older people instead of "putting them out to pasture" in a retirement center. At the same time, we are given space to be less involved, which is sometimes a little tricky for us Fellowship people who keep dreaming new dreams. We are used to thinking that we should support each other by being at all the meetings and activities. Fortunately, there is a lot of freedom for different kinds and ways of participating in the community. There's no system that tells you that you need to retire. It is so different now compared to Reba in the first decade, because early on it was mostly young people, with older people occasionally wanting to join us. Minna Regier and Dorothy Konsterlie, for instance, were in their fifties and the Stringhams well into retirement when they came to us.

We have peoplehood in a different and perhaps more real way here at Reba than what I experienced growing up. When I was a child, the Mennonites of our particular stripe were still dressing differently from the rest of the world. That made it really clear to me that we were God's people. We wore the head coverings and the women wore "cape dresses," a sleeveless vest-like-thing that we wore over a very plain dress with a lower hem than what most women wore those days. The men, when dressed up, wore "Nehru collars," which had to be tailored from "worldly suits." Wherever we went people knew who we were.

My convictions have broadened since then. A special garb is no longer important, but I am still convinced that Jesus calls us to follow a different path than the world. The upside-down kingdom is a concept that is especially significant for me. It refers to the way Jesus's value system and way of life produce an alternative culture that contrasts with the world's values and lifestyles.

**Hilda enjoying a visit with her friend Margarita
from Reba's sister community, Valle Nuevo, in El Salvador**

How I understand God's relation to the rest of the world has also changed dramatically. I feel certainty now that everyone in the world is a beloved child of God, not only Christians, but those of other faiths and no faith at all. I believe that God meets us both individually and culturally in different parts of the world and different civilizations, wherever we are. We, as Christians, are only a part of a larger thing that God is doing.

I am grateful that in these later years, with my ninety-second birthday on the horizon, and with my worn-out body needing more and more hours on my recliner, that I have precious time now for talking with folks one-on-one, thinking, studying, journaling, praying, and asking God for answers to some of those vexing biblical/theological questions that I didn't take the time to engage in adequately during my earlier years. Actually, despite the aches and pains and handicaps, I find being old at Reba kind of fun. What further adventures there will be before crossing over to the Other Side, God knows, and that's all I need for now.

Reflections on a Fruitful Life of Singleness

SALLY SCHREINER YOUNGQUIST

Speaking as a long-term female member of Reba Place Fellowship, I have always seen Hilda Carper as an encouraging role model—particularly for single women. The fact that Hilda is a woman and has always been single has not held her back from having a significant voice in the Fellowship and church where she has exercised many leadership roles. She is truly a "Renaissance woman" in the number of significant talents she has developed and freely shared over the years in the areas of children's education, music, art, household organizational skills, administration, pastoring, social justice, and mentoring.

Hilda's autobiography lifts up various traits I find worthy of closer inspection: her faith, her courageous voice, her eye for beauty, and her fruitfulness in singleness. First and most important, Hilda's walk with God has been the taproot sustaining her vigor on so many fronts. She describes her faith developing from a young age, nurtured first at home and in the church, but later deepening through her own private worship and Scripture study. She shows an early ability to ask for God's direction and be satisfied with the answer given regarding the option to work overseas five years on a curriculum project in Switzerland. Hilda has continued to listen for God's direction throughout her long and adventurous life, taking her to the margins time and time again to work with those not valued by society. Hilda has wrestled with Scripture and communed with God her whole life long, taking her ever deeper into comprehending God's merciful character. As a result, even in her late eighties, she helped RPF take a new look at interpreting Scriptures pertaining to the possibility of gay marriage and full acceptance of sexual minorities in the church.

Hilda's spiritual, intellectual, and vocational training apart from the American mainstream no doubt contributed to her ability to speak up in situations where her minority viewpoint has been needed. We see her conservative Mennonite upbringing shaping her identity as part of a people group "separate from the world." She opts for a Mennonite Central Committee assignment in Europe at a time when many of her peers were seeking marriage opportunities at home. She hobnobs with scholars and international church colleagues, dreaming with them about how to reform the Mennonite Church. She seeks out opportunities for service in inner-city communities in Detroit and Chicago, showing flexibility to be sent where needed. In an era of male-dominated leadership at RPF, she was one of very few recognized female leaders confident and respected enough to raise her voice to question or critique decisions of strong male elders. Hilda is not one to mince words if feeling disagreement or if giving a prompt "no" to others' requests. Yet I have seen her show humility and tears in owning her mistakes and seeking reconciliation where needed. For women raised to "go along to get along," Hilda presented a strong alternative role model. Yet she has been a nurturer of children, a creative cook, an excellent musician, and an innovative home-maker—all classically feminine characteristics.

One has only to look at a space designed by Hilda to see beauty, simplicity, utility, and order. She admits to enjoying the role of "nest-building," evident at the Reba Day Nursery she developed, the retreat cabin she designed and furnished at Plow Creek Farm, and her own modest bedroom in the Clearing. Her worship banners and tissue collage landscapes (duplicated for commercial greeting cards) manifest these same clean lines, original design, and eye for beauty, nurtured, no doubt, by her love of nature. Hilda's musical gifts have also contributed welcome beauty and richness to Reba's worship life over the years, in concert with other gifted and creative musicians.

It's evident in Hilda's life choices that she did not make an idol out of marriage. She did not hesitate to take a five-year assignment abroad in her marriageable twenties. She did not cling to a failing engagement to a Methodist minister turning away from his faith. And she did not appear to wallow in grief and self-pity over missing the chance to marry. Instead, Hilda's long-term collaboration with Julius and Peggy Belser, begun in the West Side Christian Parish days described in these memoirs, has continued on into her nineties through her shared living arrangement with them in the Clearing Household. Julius's, Peggy's, and Hilda's gifts have complemented each other well and have created a base of stability for many others sharing short- and long-term life at the Clearing. They formed a leadership team at the Clearing for many years, until they felt the need to raise up the next generation of leaders. They helped each other host Hilda's aging mother and Julius's aging parents when elder care was needed. Now they are modeling how givers become receivers as they take their own turns receiving elder care from fellow Clearing residents. I believe this kind of long-term partnership of a single person with a married couple is a valuable model for community members in long-term singleness to consider.

Though Hilda never married or had children of her own, she has mentored many spiritual children. Some still seek her out for one-to-one meetings in her second-floor bedroom. The same qualities that made her a good nursery school teacher helped her create a secure overnight shelter for the homeless of Evanston. God has used Hilda's heart for the hurting in fruitful paths of service that have blessed all the rest of us at Reba Place.

∽

Sally Schreiner Youngquist arrived at Reba Place Fellowship fresh from college in 1973. She has served in many capacities both within and outside RPF. She was the founding pastor of Living Water Community Church from 1995 to 2009, and RPF community leader from 2009 till 2018.

Holy Discontent

TATIANA FAJARDO-HEFLIN

My husband Chico's first recollection of Hilda Carper is of her walking up to him, pointing her finger in his direction, and asserting, "You say you care about poor people! Then *you* can help me!" Hilda did not know whether Chico already had conflicting commitments, nor did she bother to explain exactly what help she needed before she volunteered him right then and there. Thus, he and I set out to help move a mattress and other small furniture from a church member's house into the basement apartment of a mentally disabled neighbor.

We didn't know this neighbor, Jessica, or her son, then a teenager on the margins of the Reba Place Church youth group. Their apartment was sparse, dark, and dirty. Jessica seemed confused and anxious and uninterested in relating to Chico or me. After the task was completed, Hilda filled us in a bit more on her history with the family. She told us about how the teenage son had confided to her that he would sometimes walk along Sheridan Avenue, looking longingly at the big beautiful houses along the lake, imagining what it would be like to live a different life, free of the squalor and chaos of his own lot. Hilda's voice cracked, holding back tears, as she relayed this reflection. She was seventy-nine at the time, forty years past her youthful season at the West Side Christian Parish, and Hilda's heart was still breaking on behalf of the poor.

Most Christians become more set in their ways and more closed to dreaming or being challenged as they get older. Hilda never succumbed to this temptation. In fact, it seemed to me that Hilda lives with a sort of holy discontent, ever earnest in her pursuit of new challenges, always questioning, and never satisfied with "coasting." She is serious about submitting to the Spirit and always being available to God's movement. And she does not allow herself to turn a blind eye to the injustice and suffering in the world nor to waywardness or unfaithfulness in the church.

Chico and I never interacted with Jessica or her son again after that day. But the experience birthed a bond between us and Hilda that would become a cornerstone of our life at Reba and of our eventual move to the poorest town in Illinois, Ford Heights.

We came to Reba in our early twenties, both filled with a strong desire to follow Jesus to a place of poverty and suffering, praying we'd become friends and family with the people there. Hilda, at that point, had spent decades relating to vulnerable people, poor African-American families, young children, homeless men, physically-disabled and elderly people. She seemed invigorated by our calling and quickly became our strongest advocate in Reba. We marveled at the fact that a woman, now in her eighties, felt compelled to pour herself into making our vision come true.

In the months before we moved to Ford Heights, Hilda helped coordinate work days at our new house, kept us at the forefront of community prayers, organized literal and metaphorical piles of stuff to meet our needs, and sewed curtains for all our new windows. I remember her offering to make the curtains as we were talking through the long list of practicalities like rugs for the cold linoleum floors and a stove for the kitchen (which the landlord wasn't intending to provide.) Hilda said, "Oh, and you're definitely going to need curtains—that will make your house feel like a home! I'll make them!" I was surprised that something rather impractical felt so important to Hilda. Now I can see what she was like in her work at the nursery, the shelter, or in the Clearing, extending her "nesting" instincts to create a nurturing space for us and our neighbors.

I often tell people how much I appreciate Hilda's feistiness. Reba, in my experience, has a rather gentle communication culture—of which Hilda is not the norm. She is unafraid to tell it like it is, to voice corrections or challenge. I'm sure that character trait can feel scary to new arrivals in her household, but I believe it is invaluable in her ability to mentor and disciple long-term. It has also been an important balancer within RPF leadership.

After we moved to Ford Heights, we named Hilda the chairperson of our support team—not just because she was excited about us wanting to share life deeply with marginal people or had experience doing so herself, but because we knew she would not shy away from asking us hard questions or telling us straight-up when we were being foolish. Her "holy discontent" is manifested in a drive to practice her discipleship the best she can and to compel others to do the same . . . even when it means coming across like "the bad guy."

Hilda's ability to speak challenge with confidence does not mean that she dominates over other voices. When RPC spent several years re-engaging its policy on same-sex marriage, Hilda was a strong voice on the necessity of the conversation and was part of the leadership group facilitating the multi-year dialogue. She had no hesitation expressing her own strongly affirming perspective on LGBTQ inclusion and, I imagine, hoped the dialogue process could lead the whole community to share her position on the issue. But she never used her leadership role to push her own views. She encouraged deep listening, prioritizing above all that we would extend God's love to one another across a spectrum of ideologies, leading, eventually, to a "third way" position that made room for both traditional and affirming perspectives. In this I see a deep maturity. Hilda is discontent because she is in tune with the Spirit.

About a year ago, physical limitations finally led Hilda to step back from attending our support team meetings, so our relationship has transitioned to visits in her bedroom. She is nearing ninety-two and facing into the dwindling time she has left. If she were of the world, she might assume that after a life of service to others she has the "right" to wash her hands of the burdens of the church and the struggle of suffering people. Instead, she is regularly asking about our Ford Heights neighbors, emphasizing the importance of us getting regular respite and retreat, and confiding, "I always did feel like we lived too wealthy, you know." Hilda Caper is *not* of this world. And I believe she will go to the grave still filled with an ever-burning fire for God and a hunger for a church that is the hands and feet of Jesus.

Tatiana Fajardo-Heflin is married to Chico Fajardo Heflin. They are members of Reba Place Fellowship on mission to the south Chicago suburb of Ford Heights.

FOUR

Margaret Wenger Gale

Divinely Appointed Community Leader, Despite Herself

I. Growing Up Mennonite in the Shenandoah Valley

I grew up on a small farm in the Shenandoah Valley of Virginia, the fourth of six children. I was too little to be one of the big kids and too big to be one of the little kids—a typical middle child! We children mostly made our own fun and played a lot together, as we had few close neighbors. I served the role of peacemaker between my younger brother and sister. I also was known as a tomboy among the girls. My father used to say that if you couldn't find Margaret, look in the top of the highest tree. We children grew up helping with our large garden, feeding chickens, helping to care for the animals and all the other work that goes into maintaining a farm and home. I was born toward the end of the Depression. We were poor, but so was almost everyone else around us. We raised most of our food and always had our needs met.

Margaret on her Daddy's lap

Margaret, gradeschool photo

My parents were ethnic Mennonites from way back. My ancestors fled from persecution in Switzerland. We were one of a very few Mennonite families in our school. At home I was thoroughly loved and secure. At school we were persecuted some because of being conscientious objectors to war in the middle of World War II. We also dressed somewhat differently, so we never really fit in at our school. I hated looking different and being different. About seven miles south of us was Eastern Mennonite College (EMC) and a sizeable Mennonite community. I used to wish we could live there. Our church life was very much influenced by EMC in a very positive way. People from Park View (as our Mennonite community was called) attended the church adjacent to our home, built on land donated by ancestors of ours. If the doors were open, we were there. My parents lived their faith. I never heard either of them say a negative word about anyone else. Mother was gentle and kind. Father was clearly head of our home and respected by us kids. He was fair and gentle, along with being firm. Both parents were approachable and affectionate.

Education was highly valued by my parents and they sacrificed a lot to send us to a couple of years of high school at EMC, and on to college beyond. As I got out in the world, I learned that the parents and home life I took for granted was rather unusual. I have come to feel a responsibility to share the love I experienced with those around me, and it is not hard to do this because love has always been such a part of my life. One way of saying it is that my love tank was filled up as a child. I am deeply grateful! Oh yes, as a teenager I found things to judge my parents for, especially my mother. Most of those things disappeared when I became a parent myself.

I was a very sensitive child and could usually be kept in line by a firm word. It was very important to me to please my parents and teachers, so I was generally obedient. I did well in school, so I also got lots of affirmation from my teachers.

I grew up in an era of revival meetings in the Mennonite Church where hell-fire sermons were preached and altar calls were given. At a young age my parents saw that I needed some protection from that exposure because it was upsetting me. They couldn't protect me forever, and at age ten I went forward at a revival meeting—mostly out of fear, I think. Then I was baptized and joined the church. For about two years I figured I was "saved" and could relax. Then as I entered my adolescent years I realized that I was still a sinner and thus began to struggle and feel pain for a few years. Sometimes I felt "saved" and sometimes I didn't. I wasn't able to share my anguish with anyone. At the same time I was also socially shy and self-conscious. As I look back I see that I developed behaviors that were obsessive-compulsive in nature. I realized that some of this was not normal and so I feared I was mentally ill. As loving and caring as my parents were, they didn't know how to help me. I always knew their concern and felt supported by their love, and that probably helped me get through that time. In spite of it all, I continued to do well in school. As I matured in years and spiritual life I was gradually able to gain a greater degree of peace.

I worked a year after high school and then went into nurses training. During those years I deliberately looked into mental health training and was able to find some ways of dealing with my obsessive-compulsive disorder. I began to see that I could live a normal life. Through that experience I gained a sensitivity to other hurting and suffering people.

I continued to deal with being socially shy and self-conscious. I had a very good group of friends in nurses training. One time, one of my roommates gave me the gift of responding to my laments over the fact that I was socially self-conscious by saying, "Margie, you are selfish!" She pointed out that I was self-conscious because I was too concerned about how others saw me, and that if I was thinking more about them I wouldn't be thinking so much about myself. I was shocked at first because I saw myself as a caring and giving person. This was a turning point for me as I began to deliberately turn my thoughts from self toward others.

II. Called to Be a Full-Time Christian, but Where?

After graduation from nurses training and becoming a registered nurse, I worked for a year and then attended EMC to work toward a BS degree, working part-time to pay for college tuition. I took some classes that were supposed to convince me that every word in the Bible was literally true, etc. I had the idea that it was a sin to doubt, so this created some struggles. I was very serious about being a Christian, but still had a lot of fear mixed in, and now was fighting doubt as well. I had a desire to be what I considered a "full-time" Christian, which meant to me being a missionary or some such thing. I thought that because of my emotional struggles I probably couldn't handle being a missionary, so I thought maybe I would just go and live in some needy area and help as I could. I broke off one relationship because I couldn't see myself as a Shenandoah Valley farmer's wife just going to church on Sundays and Wednesday evening prayer meeting.

I studied some about religious communal living in church history, but the opinion given then was that this wasn't relevant for today. At the end of the first year of a two-year program, John and Joanna (my sister) Lehman invited me to come and spend the summer with them at Reba Place Fellowship in Evanston, Illinois, while they had their first baby. I went expecting a typical Mennonite Voluntary Service unit, so imagine my surprise when I discovered they were attempting to begin an intentional Christian community! I was greatly moved by this and decided to stay on into the fall instead of going back to EMC. I did go back for the second semester, but found my heart wasn't in it. So I returned to Reba. I believed I had found what God was calling me to do, so I became a member of Reba that fall. I felt that to be part of a Christian community was building the kingdom of God on earth and fleshing out for me what it meant to follow Jesus. It was the way God was calling me to be a full-time Christian. I saw this as a lifetime commitment.

At Reba I was introduced in a new way to the God of Love that would not cast me off for doubting his existence. In fact, I was told by folks there that unless I looked at my doubts and faced into them, I wouldn't have a very strong faith. I had to make it my own. I experienced this as a great freedom! I also learned to open up and share who I was and discovered that I was loved and accepted by all those very special people. I grew a lot socially and spiritually. I came to the place that, although I couldn't prove that God existed, I chose to base my life on that belief and in Jesus as his son. God has honored that decision and the inner conviction has grown stronger as the years go by.

III. Sent to Join the Church of Hope on Chicago's Near West Side

I was working as a visiting nurse in Chicago when David and I were married. That was an eye-opener for a country girl from Virginia! I grew a lot in coming to see what the world was really like with all its social problems and injustices.

Wedding of David Gale and Margaret Weaver

After only six months of marriage we were asked to go to Peoria Street to be part of the little church community in the inner city with the Belsers, Hilda Carper, Allan and Jeanne Howe, and Albert Steiner on Chicago's Near West Side. I discovered soon afterward that I was expecting our first child, so I resigned visiting nurse work and helped out in the life of Church of Hope. Those were very important and growing years for me. Four of our five children were born there (including twins). It was a big eye-opener for me to live there. We were in Chicago during the years of the Civil Rights movement. I remember going with others from Peoria Street to hear Dr. Martin Luther King Jr. speak at Soldier Field. After five years, urban renewal leveled the area we lived in to make way for the University of Illinois Chicago campus. Looking back, I see that I learned and received far more in that inner-city context than what I had to offer.

IV. Reba Sends Us to Help Launch Rural Plow Creek Fellowship

We moved back to Reba and settled into community life. Our fifth child was born there. It was during our last year at Reba that a vision for founding a rural community was born. Through the years, various ones had longingly talked about wanting a rural place, but it always seemed these were our desires, not of the Lord. We had the idea that the city was where the need was strongest and we should be there. As the hippie movement arrived, quite a few young people came to check out Reba Place. However, they were looking for rural communities, not the city. Suddenly it became relevant to establish a rural community to provide a Christian alternative to the communes that were springing up around the country. So Plow Creek Fellowship (PCF) was born three hours west of Chicago. That was a big leap of faith and a very exciting time! It was also a lot of hard work!

About the time when we left Reba there was a growing interest in the Holy Spirit movement. This touched an interest and a longing of mine. I went back to Reba for a meeting with Graham Pulkingham from the Church of the Redeemer in Houston. At that meeting he told the gathered body that he believed they already had the Holy Spirit, but just needed to claim this gift and act on it. I had not been there for all the meetings so I wasn't sure if I was included. I raised my hand and asked, "What about me?" Graham looked at the people there and asked them to tell him about this sister. Then he looked me in the eyes and said, "You have the Holy Spirit." And I believed him, and my spiritual experience took on a new life. Somewhere along the way I made a new commitment to spend regular time with the Lord. That was also the beginning of a growing richness in my walk with Jesus.

Another highlight for me came at a Shalom Communities Conference when I attend a workshop led by Jim Stringham called "God Wants to Speak to You, Are You Listening?" He spoke to a longing I had to better learn to hear the Lord. I began following his guidance of daily listening to

God's voice and life has never been quite the same. Out of that has come a deepening experience of God's love for me, and acceptance as his child. I am sure that having the earthly father I had was helpful to me in that too.

I remember another time when we were looking at our spiritual gifts. We were asked to identify what part of the body we were. I saw myself as "hands" and "heart." I could feel good about the heart part, but wasn't as thrilled by the hands (mundane service things I did). Then it came to me that Jesus was the master servant, and I began to feel better about my gifts. This helped me to deal with some feelings of jealousy I was having toward someone else that I saw as possessing more desirable gifts.

Two sisters from Valle Nuevo (El Salvador) visiting Plow Creek for a summer. Angelica and Erlinda share a picnic with Elsie Mast and Margaret Gale on the community green

Plow Creek members and Shalom Community visitors circle up before a meal at the Plow Creek Common Building

When Dr. Ed Johnson opened a medical clinic in Tiskilwa, I, along with Sarah Foss, Louise Stahnke, Lynn Fitz, and Donna Harnish, went to work there. That was a rich time of fellowship and serving the Tiskilwa community together. During those years I developed hip problems and had my first hip replacement surgery. I was asked to become an elder on the Plow Creek Fellowship leadership team, and after some struggle, agreed to take that on. I had grown up with only men as leaders and so had to go against my inner voice to do that. I have to admit that I often thought of myself as "sort of" an elder. During that time I took a course by mail from the Associated Mennonite Biblical Seminaries on pastoral counseling. That was a very good and affirming experience.

During those years I also began taking occasional retreats at a Catholic retreat center for spiritual direction. All of my adult life I have been a listener for many different people. This was the first time that someone listened to just me for a full hour. I was so blessed by that and realized the importance of being a good listener. I had a desire to take training as a spiritual director in order to become better prepared to listen. But the opportunity was never given, and I accepted that I was meant to be a minister in an unofficial capacity. After eleven years I felt it right to resign from being an elder.

After David retired from the building business at age seventy, he continued to do the bookkeeping for PCF and the farming operation. As the years went by I began to notice signs of mild cognitive disorder. After a slight stroke it became clear that he could no longer continue doing the books. The signs of dementia slowly increased until, in his last couple of years, he needed to give up driving and became more and more dependent on me to care for him. He also developed some heart problems and chronic obstructive pulmonary disease (COPD). Our children and Plow Creek folks were very supportive during this time.

V. Caring Well for One Another in Decline of Body and Community

After our youngest child graduated from high school, we moved to a Fellowship house in Tiskilwa to make room for families with children to live on the farm. It became clear by January of 2015 that we needed to move back to the farm so that we could have more support. Many people, including our children, former Plow Creek members, and Reba Place Fellowship, contributed towards installing an elevator at the Corner House so that we could live in the second-floor apartment. This was the house that David designed and oversaw the building of, that our family lived in for seven years in the early days of Plow Creek. Many people helped us to move to that apartment while David was in a nursing home for rehabilitation following a hospitalization. He felt very much at home there and remembered building it. It was such a gift being able to be there together in that house, looking out over the meadow, where he felt so much at home.

With the support of our family and Plow Creek folks we managed there until the difficult decision was made for him to go to a nearby nursing home. David was there only a month until his death on November 21, 2016. Although this was a difficult time, it was also a very precious time in which we became emotionally very close.

We were comforted and blessed at his memorial service, held in the Plow Creek Common Building, in the presence of many past and present members of the wider Shalom Mission Communities. A year later David's ashes were placed in a beautiful handcrafted wooden box, made by our youngest son, Tim, and buried in the Plow Creek cemetery on the property where he had lived the majority of his life, serving God and his fellow human beings.

Our family gathered in the cemetery. It was a beautiful fall day with a gentle wind blowing, rattling the leaves still on the trees. We were there for a while just being quiet together, honoring David, and together committed him back to the earth, and to his Creator. It was a blessed time, and brought needed closure. It gave me a peace beyond what I had experienced before.

Our family together designed his memorial stone with the very fitting verse from Micah 6:8.

> He has told you O mortal, what is good;
> And what does the Lord require of you
> but to do justice, and to love kindness,
> and to walk humbly with your God?

During this time of dealing with David's decline and death we were also experiencing the decline of Plow Creek Fellowship. This added to the loss that I was experiencing.

For quite a few years I had seen what was happening. Some of those committed to shared funds were leaving and those of us left were aging. The younger generation was attracted to the life in community but not to shared funds. In reality, the life at Plow Creek would not be there, or possible, without shared funds. It was clear to me that we needed to make some significant changes in our structure and life together if we were to continue. By the summer of 2009, all of those relating to Plow Creek were invited to help us reenvision Plow Creek.

That began the process that after many ups and downs ended up in the decision in 2017 to dissolve Plow Creek Fellowship. Although the decision to dissolve was painful, and I experienced it as yet another loss, I was ready for this to happen. I came to believe that we had fulfilled our calling to establish a rural community, and that in spite of many failures and sins on our part, God had blessed many people through the life here, and in ways we are still learning about. We had been faithful and God had blessed that. I do not see the ending of Plow Creek as a failure; rather that we had fulfilled our mission, and it was time to turn this land, buildings, and other resources over to others who would use it for his glory. We were supported and guided in this process over a number of years by Sally Youngquist, Allan Howe, and David Janzen from Reba Place, who spent an uncountable number of trips, hours, prayers, and effort on our behalf.

Some excerpts from my journal during this time in response to the question, "What is your vision for this place?" (I indicate thoughts that I felt were from the Lord in italics):

> The group that is left is unable to come up with a common vision or energy to carry it out. When the vision is of God the energy to carry it out is also given.
>
> *"My voice, dear one, will be quiet and peaceful. It will not have an anxious quality. Wait until you hear my still small voice in the midst of the storm."*
>
> *"Margaret, your job is to be a peaceful presence—to wait for my still small voice. It is too much for you to figure out. It is not too much for me. Smile. Quiet, my dear one. Trust me to be in charge."*
>
> *". . . your job is to hold out for a sense of peace and joy. That is how you will know. It is not your job to come up with the ideas—just to recognize my voice when you hear it and to give your anxious spirit to me. I love you! Go in peace! Also, your job is to help discern when the voice is not of me. Trust me. I am trustworthy!"*
>
> This word came to me in response to my question, "What is my role in this now? Can I retire from Community?":

> *"Smile—yes dear one, You can leave the family farm 'to the Kids,' but not community. I will give you a new community to be a part of, one that will better fit your energy and station in life."*

After the Stahnkes moved away and Sarah planned to move, too, I knew that I could no longer stay at Plow Creek. Although I affirmed the turning over of Plow Creek to Hungry World Farm (HWF), it was too painful for me to stay there and watch it happen. I applied to live in an apartment at Greenfield, a local retirement community in Princeton, and was accepted and put on a waiting list. Sarah Foss invited me to live with her until that opened up. I was there four and a half months. The time with Sarah was a great blessing. Our love and friendship grew and deepened as we were able to support and care for each other in the loss of our husbands and Plow Creek. I moved to Greenfield, where I had worked the last five years of my nursing career, and where Sarah now works, enabling us to keep in close touch.

After I lost David and Plow Creek, I experienced a time of wondering, "Now what do I do?" My life in Community and at Plow Creek had been my life's calling, and in the latter years much of my time was spent caring for David. As I prayed about this I felt the Lord "saying" to me that I was to rest and wait and he would make my path clear. I have found that at Greenfield I am able to contribute to the common life by reaching out in friendship, and that I am also ministered to. More and more as I wonder whether I am doing "all that is required." I have felt the Lord reassuring me that I do not need to be doing anything special—that being who he made me to be is what is required.

I feel so blessed by the provision that has been given to me to be here at Greenfield. It is a beautiful place to live and I marvel at the gift! I feel humbled by the realization that this is part of "all these things that will be given to you." David and I together did indeed seek first the kingdom, and I am growing in being able to accept this and give thanks. "I do not know what the future holds, but I know who holds the future, and I know who holds my hand." Now from my journal written during this time:

> Now what do I do now? Community has been my life's work. It has been my way of serving You, my way of being a Christian, of having meaning and purpose. Now how do I serve You? How do I live my life for You and not just for myself? I still want to be a full-time Christian. This is a loss that I bring to you.

After Plow Creek Church closed I began to attend Willow Springs, the local Mennonite church, along with others from Plow Creek. This has been a fairly easy adjustment for me because of a long history of relating to and cooperating with Willow Springs. I became a member there recently, along with Sarah and Jim and Meg Foxvog.

Now as I review my life, I am greatly blessed by our five children and their families. Their support helped to make it possible for David to be at home as long as he was.

Our oldest son, Eric, lives in Dixon, Illinois, about forty-five minutes north of Princeton. He is a medical doctor. He and his wife, Nancy, have four sons. Our daughter, Laurie, and husband, Bob Turner, live in Grafton, Wisconsin. She is a teacher in the public school system. Bob is a chaplain in the Milwaukee hospital system. They have four children. Steve and his wife, Jill, live in Fort Collins, Colorado. They are both psychologists. They have two daughters. Andy and his wife, Monica, live in San Diego, California. They both work as scientists in medical research. Our youngest, Tim, lives in Walnut, Illinois, about half an hour away from Princeton. Tim makes beautiful handcrafted wooden musical instruments that he sells at a booth he shares with their daughter, Jaedyn, who makes very creative handcrafted items to sell. He works part-time at a local hardware store. His wife, Carol, works as a physician assistant at a clinic in Walnut. I get to see them fairly often. Eric and family are close enough for frequent visits, are readily available, and come quickly when needed. They are all very generous with their time and resources. I am blessed!

One Sunday, on the way to meeting, I was feeling grief and pain that Plow Creek was no more. Then something happened, truly a gift from God. I found myself feeling joyful that I could be a part of giving the gift of this land and this place to Hungry World Farm—back to the one who gave it—to whom it has always belonged. I felt joyful that I could be a part of developing Plow Creek Fellowship in the first place, and now a part of giving it to HWF for his glory. This came from above—a gift of joy that I did not conjure up myself.

Margaret Wenger Gale

Margaret reclining at her Greenfield retirement center apartment in Princeton, IL, 2019

Friend to the Friendless

Sarah Foss

Determined, protective, loving, and emotional are several words to describe Margaret.

The Gales and Fosses were in the same weekly sharing group for many years, beginning in the seventies. Through the death of David Gale and my husband, Rich, right up to this day, Margaret and I get together weekly to share with each other. So when David Janzen asked me to write something about Margaret, I got tearful because she and I have a very strong bond.

In 1977, Rich and I arrived at Plow Creek expecting our first child. The Gales's oldest child was in ninth grade. Rich and I had the blessing of observing and discussing the Gales's raising of children from grade school, high school, and college, to weddings and grandparenting. What a privilege for us as we began our own family.

As Rich and I shared our most painful life experiences, we could always count on Margaret to cry with us. Her hugs and affirmation were the balm in Gilead that we needed.

The Gales's willingness to move out of their beloved Corner House to make room for the Stewarts on the farm was a great example of putting the kingdom before their own preferences. I love how God gave back that space for David's last days. While the Gales lived in Tiskilwa, Margaret was like a missionary for Plow Creek. She made friends with neighbors all over town. Now she does the same thing at Greenfield retirement center. She befriends everyone and people love her. (I work there and they tell me!)

I have observed Margaret grow in her trust in God despite a tendency in earlier years to anxiety. I believe this growth comes from her daily devotions and listening to the Lord. She is good at writing out her thoughts and feelings on a subject and then hearing and writing the Lord's response to her. I have learned so much from her by hearing what God tells her.

Her loyalty and love for David is a good model for me of love and marriage. Her care for him towards the end of his life was also a testament of devotion, love, and giving her all through a very difficult time.

As our beloved Plow Creek has ended, Margaret and I share our griefs and sorrows. What a blessing to have a dear sister living nearby, a sister who is an excellent listener, who empathizes, who cares, who shares and loves with a Christlike heart.

∼

Sarah Foss has been on the Interim Leadership Team along with Mark Stahnke (from Plow Creek Fellowship), David Janzen, and Sally Youngquist (from Reba Place Fellowship) to help wrap up Plow Creek affairs after its legal dissolution. Sarah has been writing a poem a week since the passing of her poet husband Rich Foss in January 2017. She is a nurse and friend of all the Plow Creek alumni.

Leader, but a Caring Person First

Mark and Louise Stahnke

Mark: We first met Margaret and David Gale when we arrived at Plow Creek on July 4, 1979. That's forty years ago. Back then there were more Plow Creek members than could dwell on the farm, so some of us lived a mile away in the village of Tiskilwa. Once Margaret and David's five children were grown up, they moved to the "town house" so families with children could live on the farm. This was a sacrifice, but the Gales were willing to take their turn.

Plow Creek Fellowship had some tensions with Tiskilwa residents because we hosted refugees and were pacifists. But Margaret made it her mission to be an ambassador of good will, walking to the post office every day and deliberately making friendships with neighbors. She could make friends with people who had different political views, something the rest of us were not so good at.

Margaret's compassion showed in her frequent tears when she talked in sharing times about the needs of other people and about issues of justice around the world. Her stability and gentleness were rooted in a daily practice of meditating on Scripture, listening to the Lord, and journaling. Margaret had a great gift of summing up a community conversation, expressing our consensus in a faith-filled way because she had been listening so well. In so doing, she never pushed an agenda of her own. She did not like to be a spokesperson or a leader, but she always had the big picture in mind and could articulate our purpose as disciples of Jesus in community as well as anyone in the Fellowship.

Already in 2008, Margaret spoke up about some trends at Plow Creek that had her concerned about its long-term survival. So in 2017, when it came time to "close up shop," she could graciously lead us by saying, "It is time to end and to end well. God is pleased with the community's faithfulness over forty-six years. Furthermore, Plow Creek was not a failure; its work is simply done."

∽

Louise: I worked with Margaret for ten years as part of the team of four nurses who staffed the Plow Creek Clinic in Tiskilwa along with Dr. Ed Johnson back in the seventies and eighties. Margaret was fastidious about cleanliness, so it worked best for her to be in charge of sterilizing the equipment while I took care of the administration. She had her tidy and efficient systems—"Don't talk to me, I'm counting pills." For decades, until a few years ago, Margaret and I have prayed together every week. In praying for people's needs we could also see what to do about them. Some said that "Margaret and Louise hold the community together."

Margaret and David Gale complemented each other. He delighted in his children jumping off the house roof into a snow drift. Margaret fretted but also flexed with the situations. David was able to organize the community in workdays and large building projects. He knew how to help children have a high time shingling a roof alongside of adults with no one falling off. Margaret was forever proud of what David had accomplished in building up the homes and large common building with room for fifty community members who lived together, at our peak.

Margaret saw herself as a caring person first rather than a leader. But the community really needed her leadership gifts. She was a stabilizing influence among some often disruptive people.

Here's one last story about Margaret's compulsive cleanliness and her willingness to flex, nevertheless. Her youngest son, Tim, would often bring critters home from the woods and the creek, and enjoy them as pets in the house. One time he brought home a nest of eggs which he wanted to hatch. It turned out that they were snake eggs. The brood of vipers had to go, Margaret decreed, except for one that was allowed to stay in its box. But this pet kept escaping and showing up in various places around the house. Finally, it stopped showing up. Was it dead, gone, or still lurking somewhere? Twenty years later, when Margaret and David moved back from town to their old family home, their children pitched in money to buy them an elevator and some new kitchen cupboards. When they tore out the old base cabinets, there on the floor laid the skeleton of a dead snake—a reminder of the uneasy yet loving tension between a budding zoologist child and a cleanliness-driven mom, now reconciled in the gift of a new kitchen and an old pet's final revelation.

Last week (beginning of January 2019) we drove from Goshen, Indiana, to pick up Margaret in Princeton, Illinois, so she could share a few days with us. Margaret used to never complain, but now she admits that she has some hard days. But her faith is strong. We miss each other. We are so glad that Sarah Foss is Margaret's nurse in an assisted care facility. We're grateful that we "Old Creekers" are still finding ways to care for one another even though our former Plow Creek Fellowship is no more.

Mark and Louise Stahnke, who lived almost forty years at Plow Creek Fellowship, now reside in retirement with their son David, in Goshen, Indiana. For many years, Mark was a social worker and Louise a baker and head of hospitality at Plow Creek.

FIVE

Albert Steiner

Geek (before There Were Geeks)
with a Heart for God and His Nation

I. Growing Up a Depression Kid

I was born on a farm in Ohio during the Depression. My mother was my father's second wife after his first wife died of cancer. She had been teaching school and was actually older than my father by a few years. He had two children, a son and a daughter, by his first wife. My parents were married in 1934, in the middle of the Great Depression. I was born about a year and a half after they were married, in the middle of a big snow storm—so big my parents couldn't get to the hospital. Instead, Dr. Yoder came and delivered me at home. I was named Albert Jonas Steiner II after my grandfather Albert J. Steiner, a Mennonite minister and bishop.

Albert Steiner at about four years old, "driving" a horse team and sled

Dad was a minister who went to Goshen (Indiana) seminary for one year. Then the money ran out. My mom had thought she would be able to sew dresses for other people at Goshen, and that she'd be able to pay for our family living there. But nobody else at Goshen had money to buy handmade dresses, so instead of being there two years they were there just one year. The strongest memory for me from those days was when my younger sister, Joanna, and I were supposed to watch our youngest brother, Daniel, and while we weren't watching he went for a walk. He was eventually found on Eighth Street about ten blocks from home, which was a very scary thing.

When I graduated from high school, I had a sports jacket to go with a tie for my graduation picture. Later, we noticed that my older brother had graduated from high school with the same sports jacket. That illustrates how we reused everything we could.

Dad was a lay minister, though that's not what Mennonites called it at the time. They didn't pay their ministers; rather they took ministerial support offerings maybe once a quarter, but that was only minimal help, so Dad was also a schoolteacher and we had a farm to help make ends meet. We had some milk cows, so we got money from selling milk. Father drove with big boxes of eggs for resale to some stores in Youngstown. That's how we got cash. As far as I can remember, Dad was always about a thousand dollars in debt to several lenders.

Three times Dad had nervous breakdowns. Soon after he married my mother he had an episode. There weren't any psychological services available at the time, so my father's father told my mother that she needed to accompany her husband all the time, and keep him going, doing all the farm work he needed to do. With that process of support from my mother, he came back out of it. Father always had difficulty confronting people, which is something I certainly learned too well from him.

We have a picture of me at about three years old on a sled with some horses. By the time I helped with farm work, we had gotten rid of the horses and had a small John Deere H tractor. But in the shed, we still had all the horse-drawn equipment: plows and, in the barn, a wagon for occasional use. We raised a rotation of corn, wheat, oats, and hay with alfalfa. The alfalfa was a legume that put nitrogen back into the soil so that when corn was raised the next year, the soil was more fertile. I remember staying home from school to plow fields and at other times to cultivate corn while my father taught school. I know we also used commercial fertilizer, so it wouldn't exactly have been called an organic farm at that point. We raised feed that went to the chickens and cows. The chickens would have been what you call free-range.

I remember working and learning alongside my dad, who knew how to install water pipes and run electricity, so I got pretty good at that. I wasn't so good at carpentry, which my younger brother excelled at. I didn't have the patience for it. I've always tended to be the kind of person who just "did it" and only read the manual if I got into trouble, whether it was with toys, or later with computers and software. For household equipment I would read the manual before I went forward with it, because there were too many danger alerts as to what could go wrong.

During World War II, pacifism was important to me. This was my faith, the way I grew up. This unpopular stance isolated me from a lot of the school kids, especially the bully types, but I don't remember any actual physical threats. There were a number of other Mennonites in school, so I wasn't totally alone. But even then I was a loner. It was easier for me to relate to books and ideas and thoughts than to people. So that was how I grew up. I was sort of a lonely geek.

II. In College: Training to Become a Pastor

I made a Christian confession at the age of ten at a revival meeting at our home church. Some outside preacher had come in to preach. For the next ten years I had an up-and-down Christian life. When I went to summer camp, I would be called back to follow Jesus more seriously. I went to college planning to be a minister, something I felt I ought to do. I would have been the seventh generation of Steiner pastors. So I took sociology, pre-seminary Bible, and Greek. My junior year I decided to go to Eastern Mennonite College because I heard there was a good sociology professor, Paul Peachy. That proved to be a very moving experience. Paul Peachy was part of the Concern Group which issued a series of Anabaptist pamphlets and was, in many ways, the ideological base out of which Reba Place Fellowship developed. I also took his class in ecclesiology, the study of the nature of the church. That's where I came to see the church as the body of Christ, a communal group of disciples with a mission in the world.

There were no student loans in those days. I got a $100 scholarship for being a minister's kid. Other than that, I worked summers at a hardware store. I worked another summer at the feed mill where my brother had been employed. At college I had a variety of jobs washing dishes, running projectors, and working in the library. And as far as I can remember I never worried about money. I seemed to have just enough for my needs.

From my junior year on I was in touring choirs; at Eastern Mennonite College and then at Goshen. I liked music. I liked to sing. I had one course in music that helped me understand the basics like sight-reading, harmony, and structure.

III. Learning to Live in the Inner City at Church of Hope

For my senior year I came back to Goshen College, where I found like-minded people meeting together with a professor named John Miller at his house. There we talked about how the Mennonites should become an intentional Christian community, more like the early church in Acts 2. Our group was controversial. During that year John Miller was given a leave, which was supposed to teach him how to get practical and leave off telling students about the communal nature of the early church. This "exile" turned out to be the birth of Reba Place Fellowship. John and Louise Miller were joined by John and Joanna Lehman from Eastern Mennonite College (now University) where I'd studied, and Ted Hartsough, another Goshen student. With some help from the Mennonite Central Committee, which at that time was run by John Miller's father, Orie Miller, the community bought its first house at 727 Reba Place in Evanston, Illinois. The group at that time was organized as an MCC voluntary service unit.

The next year, after Reba Place started, I explored coming to Reba Place for the summer. Reba had some contact with Julius Belser, who was then at the Church of the Brethren Seminary in Chicago. Julius was a part of the West Side Christian Parish, a group of pastors who shared their incomes and had significant shared life together in ministry. Julius had a vision of being the church in one of the poorest neighborhoods in the West Side of Chicago. His vision was to call people to a life of discipleship with Jesus, and to build a committed life together in an interracial context. That seemed pretty close to what Reba Place was interested in, so Reba and Julius sponsored a summer children's project in Chicago, near where Julius was starting the little Church of Hope. I joined in this group of five volunteers living in what's called a "cold-water flat" on Peoria Street. Our rent was $35 a month. We had a kitchen with one cold-water faucet, a living room, and another small room just big enough to put in a set of bunk beds.

We were in a tough neighborhood, but we were in the back of the building accessed through a dark transom way, so dark that none of the toughs from the neighborhood cared to follow us because they didn't know what they'd run into back there. I never had anything stolen from me, though one of the other guys had a watch taken off of his wrist. One night, however, I had gone to chapel on the next street to get the community checkbook. I had on a raincoat because it was cool, so I held the checkbook inside the coat. As I walked back to Roosevelt Road a young Black man started walking beside me. I think he didn't expect to see a "whitey" in that neighborhood and was thinking of robbing me. The way I held on to the check book he might have thought I was holding a gun. I just kept walking, not showing any fear, till finally, as I approached Roosevelt Road, a more lit up place, he stopped walking beside me, for which I was much relieved.

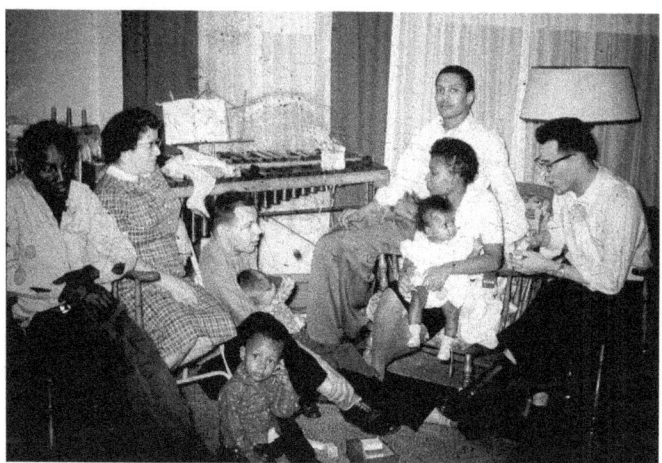

Small group meeting of Church of Hope
Albert is on the floor in the middle

Church of Hope was a terrific learning experience for me. I had grown up in a farm culture, which even carried over to college. But here I was plopped into the center of a big and complex city. As part of the West Side Christian Parish, we heard various speakers talk about Chicago, its politics, its social and economic structures. We were in a "port of entry" for poor African Americans migrating from the South. Those already in that neighborhood were either very poor and hadn't been able to move out, or they'd moved up recently from somewhere in the South. Many were on welfare, mostly women with children. It was on the West Side that I learned about the anger that resulted from the various kinds of discrimination African Americans experienced. In my high school there were children from one African-American family. At Goshen College I knew a few people of color, but I never had much contact with them. So this was a new encounter with an entirely different culture. I was learning from people who were very honest about how they felt. We encountered the rage that young people carried over the lack of opportunity they encountered, the discrimination, the hostile police—it was just a hard scene.

Initially, with five guys at Peoria Street, we ate suppers together. I remember making big bowls of casserole—I'd throw in stuff like beans, potatoes, corn, and tomatoes, and put it on the stove. We seemed to get along OK. It was a good time. If we wanted to shower, we had to go over to the Y because ours was a cold-water flat. It was an old place which previously had been a fancy house. The floors had been divided into smaller apartments. The main thing we learned was how to survive in this urban, interracial setting.

After the end of the summer, some of the volunteers returned to school or other pursuits. This would have been the summer of 1958, the year after Reba Place started.

Conrad Wetzel and I continued to live in the apartment at 1221 Peoria Street. I had a job running projectors and helping with audio visual equipment at Roosevelt University. This was my first Chicago job and I had an African American as boss. Later I had a job with the National Opinion Research Corporation associated with the University of Chicago. I'd take the bus out to whatever block they wanted me to survey, and I'd count housing units. I remember riding the bus to odd places in the city, counting the housing units on the block so that other people could interview every nth household.

This was during the Vietnam War and there was a draft. I chose to start my alternative service as a conscientious objector to war. The first year I washed test tubes and did lowly work at a clinic of the University of Chicago Hospitals. The second year I was assigned to participate in the neighborhood program of Church of Hope. I was supposed to approach parents on Peoria Street and ask if they would let their children go to a summer camp the church was sponsoring. But I found that I simply could not go up and talk to people and ask them for something, much like my father. It took some really hard soul-searching, talking with John Lehman and a psychologist, Dr. Hobart Mowrer, and other people to realize that

I wasn't going to become a pastor. I did not have the social confidence to even ask people for something.

I decided to try the path of physics in which I had done very well in high school, ranking ninth in the state of Ohio. I began to study science at University of Illinois, Navy Pier. After the first semester I needed to go to Champaign-Urbana for more courses since I had lots of math to make up. I landed student employment in the physics department writing computer code to interpret the curved paths of particles in cloud chambers downstream from the atom smasher at Argonne National Labs near Chicago. I really, really liked computers, which were a totally new thing when there were only a few of them in the country.

For two and a half years, I studied at the University of Illinois in Champaign-Urbana. At first I attended a silent Quaker Meeting for Sunday Worship but eventually found it too silent and theoretical. Then I found a Salvation Army post with a Sunday Meeting of mostly lower-class persons. It was a good time there for me. I often led out in the Sunday School times for adults. I gained a lot of respect for the Salvation Army, but left after the Colonel gave me the "honor" of carrying the American Flag to the front of the church. I didn't say anything about carrying the flag, but I felt it was much too nationalistic. It was part of my weakness to say nothing, but after that I never went back.

Around that time, I moved in with Conrad Wetzel and his wife, Martyne, and went with them to the Brethren Church. Conrad and Martyne were members of Reba Place on mission for Conrad to get a PhD. After the University of Illinois at Champaign-Urbana, I ended up studying at the University of Chicago and then at Northwestern University.

For a time, I worked at the Cook County welfare department in the admissions office, interviewing people who came in wanting assistance. I had to do two to four interviews an hour. I'd write down what they told me and then take it all to my supervisor. She'd look it over, maybe ask me some questions, say more things I had to find out, and then she would approve or disapprove of this particular applicant for welfare. I learned a fair amount about people and bureaucracies doing that work for a year.

During all this time my church membership remained with the interracial Church of Hope on Chicago's West Side. For a time, I kept books for the Church of Hope intentional community. We had common funds between White members who, as an expression of solidarity, lived on the same income level as the welfare recipients in the church. Julius and

Peggy Belser taught us how to "make do" with little in the urban context. I remember driving the Belser VW van and entering Lower Wacker Drive where I needed to turn on the headlights. But the headlight knob was missing, so we used a beer can opener to turn the stem. When I reached for the opener, I fumbled it, and it fell down through a hole in the floorboards onto Wacker Drive. I had to make my way though the dark till I came back up to daylight. That's the kind of high-class vehicles we had.

IV. In the Civil Rights Movement—Five Eye-Opening Days in the Albany, Georgia, Jail

While I was still working for Cook County Welfare, and just before I started classes at University of Chicago, a delegation of clergy and laity went down to Albany, Georgia, to stand with Martin Luther King Jr. and the civil rights movement at that time. I asked to terminate my job a week early so I could take part in that. Before I went, I bought a cheap suit on Maxwell Street for $10. Our members at the Church of Hope approved of and encouraged me to make this trip as a witness against the social deprivation to which African Americans had been subjected for generations. They sent me with a $200 check to pay my bail. When we arrived, Dr. King wasn't there at the church, but Andrew Young met us. We went downtown and we stood in front of the courthouse to pray for justice. The police told us we had to disperse and we didn't, so they hauled us off to jail. I think it was an all-White delegation. We were imprisoned in a small space with about fifteen bunk beds.

I was told that one might smuggle a Bible into jail by tucking it in the back of your shirt while they were taking your belongings, so I did that. At some point we decided to express our protest by fasting. We didn't go in for any meal as long as we were there, which was about five days. A few people paid their bail and left early as they had certain obligations.

The main thing I learned from that experience came from talking with two rabbis in our group. I learned from them about the frightful persecution of Jews in Europe, particularly around Easter time. They feared being mobbed or shot as "Jesus killers." I also learned how much Christians intensely persecuted the Jews both before and during World War II. They had every reason to fear Christians and fear the message of Christ. That's something I'd never heard before, growing up as I did in the country.

Similarly, I'd never heard of the kind of persecution suffered by African Americans, both personally and structurally. I learned how the police were much more likely to arrest them, how they were excluded from the jobs or housing they wanted. All in all, the experience at Peoria Street, and going down to Georgia, really opened my eyes to a whole new culture of deprivation I'd never heard of growing up where I did. I'd been trying to tell these sinners that Jesus loved them and they needed to repent to receive God's salvation, but I started to realize that the need for repentance, salvation, and God's forgiveness applied to me for my sins also.

Following our five days of fasting, I was in no condition to ride a bus back to Chicago. I was dropped off at Koinonia Farms (near Americus, Georgia) where they showed me how to break my fast and recuperate. Later I returned to volunteer at Koinonia for a month and a half, and I remember many important conversations with Clarence Jordan, the community's founder and widely known public speaker for racial reconciliation. At the time there were about fifteen White people in intentional community at Koinonia, but we worked and ate alongside many Black neighbors with whom we found mutual support in community. At that time Koinonia was under a boycott from White businesses in the county. I remember going to town once to get a part for a tractor, and the dealer questioned me—where was I, a northerner, living, then he sent me away without selling me the part.

V. My Courtship with Carol Begins as Church of Hope Passes Away

In those days, Carol Huddleston, who lived at Reba Place, and I started dating. Carol would come down by "L" train and bus to the West Side on Saturday nights and then teach Sunday school at Church of Hope the following Sunday morning. We'd spend Saturday evening listening to "The Midnight Special" on WFMT. Then she'd stay overnight in the apartment with Jeanne and Hilda. We were married on the last day of 1966.

I preached on Sundays at Church of Hope for a time. Allan Howe was in seminary and Julius had moved to Reba because of illness. Only a few people came; there was no sense of connection remaining with the West Side Christian Parish. I remember preaching a funeral sermon, but I did not have the nerve to ask for a ride to the cemetery so I was not present at the burial. The undertaker did the committal.

Soon the University of Illinois exercised eminent domain and took over the neighborhood to build a new campus. As the Church of Hope was dissolved, the remaining White members moved to Reba Place. None of the Black members considered moving with us, nor did the White members talk about moving to another place nearby where we could stay together. We were exhausted. The end of Church of Hope revealed how deep were the divides that remained between the original Black members on Peoria Street and we who had moved there on mission. The division was a reminder of our society's unfair distribution of wealth and opportunity. Although we had chosen to live with limited finances in one of the worst Chicago slums, we always had the option to choose to live in a good neighborhood with trees, good roads and houses, where our neighbors knew and understood us, but our African-American friends' choices were limited economically and by prejudice and restrictions both social and legal.

When the White members of Church of Hope moved to Reba Place Fellowship in Evanston, I don't remember any celebration of our transfer. Our level of collaboration was such that Reba regarded us as members in mission who were returning home.

VI. Finding Help for My Low Self-Esteem

Growing up, I was impressed by my father as a pastor. At the same time, I inherited some of the same weaknesses—a low sense of self-worth and an inability to confront other people when it was needed. Like him, I didn't believe people would have any reason to listen to what I asked of them. The help I got for my low self-esteem came in several steps. The first source of support came from lots of counseling I received all along my journey in community.

A second step came when Allan Howe gave me a book that we read together titled *Sit, Walk, Stand*, by Watchman Nee, a powerful Christian teacher from China. This book gave me a strong sense of self-worth grounded in how God sees and values me—something no one can take away.

A third step came from Reba's participation in the Charismatic Renewal in the late sixties and early seventies. I had gone with Julius to several area meetings of the renewal and felt called to it. Then when Graham Pulkingham, from Church of the Redeemer in Houston, visited and spoke to us all at Reba about the baptism of the Holy Spirit, I became much more aware of the joy of being in relationship with Jesus. It felt natural to express this joy in worship and ecstatic prayer. At times I was given the gift of speaking in tongues and offering spontaneous prophecy.

VII. How My Career in the Field of Computers Supported Reba and Our Family

I started work at the University of Chicago computing center while still at Church of Hope. I got into the field at a time when there were only a few mainframe computers in the whole world. I started at the University of Chicago essentially as the systems manager for that computer. It was relatively new on campus. There were only tape drives, no disk drives of any kind, and we even shut the computer down for an hour at lunch. Computer programs were stored either on cards to be compiled or on tapes.

The income that I earned was a significant gift to the community, involving work that was personally interesting and generally useful. I was able to study new technologies and change from one specialty to another as opportunities opened up. I was good enough at the job so that I could develop into new specialties as the field of Internet computing grew at the university level. For example, I was network manager at Northwestern when the first connection to University of Wisconsin in Madison was made at the blinding speed of 56 KBS. I was part of the growth of the new "Internet" that first connected universities and participated in the development of the techniques and hardware that were needed to keep the Internet working without failures. I helped develop ways to find information at many other places and worked out a structure for standards so equipment at many different companies could work together in the same Internet.

I rode to work with a professor who lived in the next block and then rode Chicago busses and elevated trains back to Evanston. I was glad I could earn and contribute my paychecks to Reba Fellowship rather than feeling responsible for various kinds of ministry carried on by the Fellowship. However, for a few years, I did the bookkeeping for the three Fellowship small groups, the nursery school, our housing, and other miscellaneous funds using the computer at Northwestern University for which I was system manager. I had a program at that time on computer cards, and I punched a card for each expense, then ran the lot through the computer and got a printout that I brought to the leadership meetings. I worked for Northwestern University for forty-two years, retiring in 2010 at age seventy-four.

Because of my income, I was able to sign as guarantor of the loans for some of the buildings we bought, and for about fifteen years I was chairman of the Stewards committee that managed our property. I was officially the "president" of the Reba Place Fellowship Corporation. I was a member of the leadership of the Living Hope sector of Reba Place Fellowship, but not a leader of the entire Fellowship.

VIII. Marriage with Carol, Our Needs, and Our Growth

Carol Huddleston marries Albert Steiner on the last day of 1966

When I married Carol on December 31, 1966, we stated in our wedding vows that we would need the help of God and of our brothers and sisters in Christ. Little did we know the depth of struggles that would be part of our marriage. The first three years of our marriage went pretty well, but there were some little problems that later grew to be big problems. Our first apartment was the rear second floor of 726 Monroe, with John and Louise Miller living on the first floor. Carol found Louise a very helpful mentor both in how to be a wife and a mother. Our daughter, Karen, was born March 12, 1969.

Along the way, when we had conflicts I spent time thinking, maybe grumbling, but eventually trying to hear the Lord, and ask what he wanted me to learn from what Carol said. I also came to thank the Lord for Carol, and to find specific things and actions to thank God for. I also worked to see how to commend myself for the things I learned and ways I was improving in our interactions. We read books together about loving. We talked together about our issues and we received a lot of help listening to counselors who referred us back to listening to the Lord.

I had problems because I didn't know how to deal with conflict and anger. I would retreat into silence and sometimes sullen acceptance of a request rather than saying how I disagreed, or even that I disagreed.

About three years after the birth of our daughter, Karen, Carol started to have flashbacks of traumatic memories. I was part of the conversations with John and Joanna Lehman about these new memories. Sometimes our conflicts got worse, and I retreated even further into silence. Throughout our struggles, we continued to have a lot of love for each other, and that love was an important part of enabling us to do the slow, heavy work of facing our own problems.

When Karen was about four, we moved to 727 Reba Place, to allow another household to form where we had been living. We were informed of the move by a phone call while on a trip to visit my parents. Although this was quite a surprise, we were willing to move for the good of the Fellowship program as a whole.

In that era almost everyone in the Fellowship was living in large, extended households. We moved into a household led by Russ and Pat Harris. Carol wanted help mothering Karen. From her mother she had learned what not to do, but did not know how to mother in ways that she felt good about. I wanted to learn how to deal with the conflicts in our marriage. Early on in our time in the household there were some significant problems, but we did not consider moving out. The household introduced us to a wide variety of social experiences. For me, there were some good experiences in taking more responsibilities, having more confidence in my own decision-making, and in taking more responsibility as a husband. But I completely missed how bad the experience was for Carol. The hours I worked, 6:00 a.m. to 3:00 p.m., along with meetings every night except for Saturday, did not leave me with time for the "softer side of our marriage." Carol worked outside of RPF twenty hours a week and about thirty hours a week in the household, which left her with little time for caring for our family needs as well as the "softer side of our marriage."

I did not feel that we were a strong enough family to leave the household. At some point John Lehman became involved again with us, and a way was found for us to move out of household into an apartment of our own at 710 Monroe with Carol no longer working outside the home but caring for our home and for Karen. I continued to work full-time at Northwestern University, and had some responsibilities with Fellowship committees.

I felt that I had really failed in caring for Carol, that I had not understood how bad the experience in the household had been for her. All these problems were aggravated by the problems we carried from our pasts. During this very difficult time the Lord taught me humility, how to ask for forgiveness, and how to face my own failures and to move on from there with the Lord's grace and forgiveness.

I have had a long time of growing and learning to be more open with Carol, and learning to thank the Lord for the gifts that he gives me through Carol. Within the context of Reba Place Fellowship, I am learning to be more intimate with myself, with Carol, and with God. As I age, I am able to do less and less for others and am learning to accept that my worth is from God's love, not from what I can do.

Albert and Carol with daughter Karen and her children, Kyle and Kristin

We continue to need professional Immanuel Prayer sessions every month. Often these counseling times are very difficult, but they also bless our lives and bear good fruit in our life together. They help us see how much Jesus loves us and is with us in the painful circumstances of life. The Lord has blessed us to hear each other better, to speak our needs and concerns without fear or shame.

IX. Looking Back, Looking Ahead

In my retirement years I felt called to explore some of my earlier theological assumptions, to make sure that what I believed comes from my own experience of hearing the Lord. Some of this exploration started when I interacted with a friend who had been a Christian but was now a Buddhist, and who took yearly pilgrimages to be part of a teacher's community in the mountains of India. When I wondered how to talk to my friend about Christianity, I felt a nudge from the Lord to listen. This friend had heard all the Christian arguments—there was no use in going over them again. Instead, I needed to hear him out with an open heart, and verbally respond with gladness to the parts of his experience I could resonate with. Convincing someone of the good news was in God's hands. My task was to be a listening friend, and to honestly share what the Lord had done for me, to admit what the Lord was still working on me, and to leave the outcome in God's hands. As I tried to do that with him, it became clear that this was the call for me in relating to all of my friends. To listen respectfully and with gladness, to share honestly about my failures and pains, as well as what was going well between me and the Lord, and acknowledge the places the Lord was helping fix up in my life.

I started to explore a faith inspired by a "critical realism" view of the Bible rather than the inerrant view I'd absorbed as I was growing up. I had always been bothered by the contradiction between the pacifism of Jesus and the violence that God seemed to approve of in the Old Testament. I appreciated reading Eastern Mennonite Seminary professor Ted Grimsrud on this theme, but then worked out my own understanding of "the wrath of God." Two moves in this story for me were the plagues in Egypt as part of the exodus, the wilderness journey, and the murderous invasion of Palestine. Second was the horrific violence of the Babylonian invasion of Judea. And then, two generations later, under Ezra and Nehemiah, some Jews returned to Judea and reclaimed Palestine from those who had moved into the vacant lands. To me it seemed that "the wrath of God" was his tough love. His love was for everyone, but the God who sent his only Son to be crucified for humanity's sin was also willing to discipline the people he called. God was preparing a distinctive and disciplined nation that the Messiah would lead in the redemption of the whole world.

I've also found significant inspiration in N. T. Wright's four-book series, in which *The Victory of God* stands out for me. I grew up with a very fundamentalist theology where there was no room for contradictions or historical errors in the Bible. N. T. Wright, with his critical realism, interprets Scripture according to the worldview of the writer, the worldview of the reader, and the worldview of the larger society that surrounds them. I can see how Scripture was given to make sense to the people who first received it, and this permits me to work with the conflicting perspectives I find in the Bible. Rather than selecting portions of the Bible as "rules for human life" and then imposing them on myself and everyone else, we can ask "What would Jesus do?" in our context and experience his leading here and now.

Jesus came in a time when Israel considered itself still in exile because of the Roman occupation. The nation was out of joint because they did not have the freedom to live and worship as God's nation should do. In that context, Jesus came as the Messiah, the charismatic, God-endowed leader who led the people of God out of exile, into the freedom to fulfill God's will in loving communities. The powers of evil could not stop the resurrection and Pentecost, the coming of the nation of God in his discipleship community.

These many years of counseling in our community allowed me to face my weaknesses with a lot more trust than I could have had with any outside helper. It has made a big difference that friends and acquaintances in community accepted me without judgment and trusted me with many responsibilities. I had people with whom I could rejoice as fellow pilgrims on the journey to become the nation of God, with Jesus in charge. I was part of a people willing to do anything the Lord asked us to do, rather than taking our cues from the society around us. Community has been a big source of healing, faith, and courage for me.

In recent times, I have been laying down certain community responsibilities with the trust that God will use some of the younger brothers and sisters to carry those tasks. For nine years, in my spare time, I've been developing a computer game called "Star Traders," but I may not have the energy and memory needed to finish it.

My younger sister died from cancer, my younger sister-in-law will probably die from lung and brain cancer within a year. Death is no longer a distant possibility—it is now a current likelihood. Two of my friends have forms of dementia and memory loss. I have no guarantee that I will retain my memory either.

I no longer have the energy to care for myself and Carol as I used to, so I need to rely on others. To me, loss of functionality would be harder to face than death itself. I remind myself that every breath is a gift of God. Our "Circle of Care" and our weekly twenty-hour-plus helper are my evidence of the care of the Fellowship, that I can count on them to love me when I can no longer care for myself and Carol. For me, at this time, this is part of what it means to belong to the nation of God.

Loyal Servant of the Common Good

Jeanne Howe

Though we were both affiliated in some way with the West Side Christian Parish, I had little direct contact with Albert Steiner in those years. I knew he lived with the Gales and Hilda Carper, next door to the Belsers and their household so they could look out for each other. But by the time I became a member of the Church of Hope, Albert was already a student at the University of Illinois in Champaign-Urbana. Since the early eighties we have found ourselves in the same small group at Reba Place Fellowship, and still are.

What has most impressed me about Albert Steiner is his loyalty, which was expressed in his commitment to the common purse. In the early seventies, Albert was hired by Northwestern University to help manage their new computer center because he was already a computer expert with years of training and experience. He was, in fact, the only person they interviewed for the job. At that time, and for many years since, Albert had the largest salary of anyone in the Fellowship, which he shared eagerly because he was enthusiastic about our common life and mission.

I've noticed that whatever Albert does, he is curious and educates himself in it to a high level of expertise. Through all the developments in the computer field over the decades, he has mastered the changes and kept up with his responsibilities managing computers and teams of coworkers at the Northwestern computer center until his retirement a decade ago.

I've also been impressed by Albert's care for Carol in her emotional and physical needs. Over the years she has been increasingly shut-in because of severe environmental allergies, so Albert helped set up the kind of air filtration system that she needs. When Carol could no longer attend church or Fellowship meetings, Albert engineered a sound system that allowed Carol to hear us from her living room. Later, she participated by video feed, with Albert at the camera. And now the same system works for the other disabled elders in our community.

Even though Albert has been an expert in technical matters, his vision for life and faith has been broad. Rather, he remains a radical disciple of Jesus and a cheerleader for peace and social justice concerns, supporting others who can lead out in those areas. He has been a faithful chairperson of the Reba Place Fellowship Stewards group for decades, giving oversight to the management of apartment buildings, houses, and other properties that generally serve an affordable housing mission. In every community, someone has to do those behind-the-scenes jobs with diligence, and Albert is willing to do them for us all. He has become a disciplined, self-motivated, loyal, and persistent servant of the common good for Jesus's sake.

Among many other roles at Reba (see her memoir), Jeanne Howe has been Reba Place Fellowship's office manager and has given full-time care to her husband, Allan Howe, who has Lewy body dementia.

Techy Friend, Father Figure, and Coworker

BILL CASTLE

In about the year 2000, Albert invited me to join the Reba Place Fellowship Stewards group which functioned at the time as Reba's board and oversight team for Reba's housing and other community matters. Albert was chair of the Stewards. The way he led us caught my attention; it was a servant leadership style with no ego attachment. He was excellent at asking good questions, always trying to think through how things work. His questions helped us gather the information we needed to make good decisions. He was curious, thoughtful, and smart. Carol, Albert's wife, loved to tell that in his older years Albert would go to trade conferences and lament that he could no longer listen to lecturers and read papers at the same time.

My own style in meetings was to avoid conflict, so when there were tensions in the air, I watched how Albert asked good questions rather than making assertions. I'd also get irritated over people who come to meetings without reading the background information ahead of time. You could count on Albert to do his homework.

I knew Albert many years before I learned that he had a terrible problem with headaches. Sometimes it took him a while to get his questions or comments out. Now I understand why.

I'm sobered by the sacrifices Albert made to care for his wife, Carol, and her severe chemical and environmental sensitivities. He had to engineer and keep up the systems of water and air filtration to meet Carol's needs. He was able to give Carol support and encouragement to make their marriage work well. I feel a lot of respect for Albert because of this.

My relationship with my own father was distant. Because he worked seven days a week, he was unavailable and disengaged. So I really appreciated

Albert's steady presence and attentive spirit in my life. He's been an available father figure for me to find healing and confidence.

At the Vogelback Computer Center at Northwestern University where Albert worked for almost all his career, he went back and forth between tech and management, between programming and supervising. In his last years at NU Albert was the key person in designing and upgrading security systems that made sure ten thousand persons or groups had proper access to their data, and unauthorized parties did not.

Geeky people, like Albert and myself, tend to only talk about techy stuff. While Albert can dig deep into technical problems, he also knows how to live with wider horizons. He is not gregarious, but he maintains warm and substantial relations with many people. He likes to read theology and delve into biblical history with the same problem-solving attention he brings to his regular work. He loves technical stuff, but he's even more invested in his faith and his people.

Albert was never very athletic, but he would bike or walk two and a half miles to work rather than take the train or the car. Now after knee and back surgery, he has persisted with the exercise machine in his house since he can't do the miles outside.

I think it is amazing that Reba is still here and functioning after sixty years. This is the result of lots of grace from God. But Albert's generation has modeled how to desire and pursue unity, to take responsibility for mistakes, and to value relationships more than personal positions. Time will tell if the next generations have absorbed those lessons.

Bill Castle has been a computer programmer for most of his working life. Now, he is semi-retired, serving as the RPF treasurer who issues regular financial reports containing both charts of relevant numbers and an expression of gratitude that we owe God for the provision of our needs through the community of goods.

SIX

Allan Howe

Many Gifts Communally Forged into Christlike Service

I. Childhood: Learning about Sin and Injustice

At three years of age, I knew something was wrong with the sight I saw. A dust-coated donkey was tied by a rope to the back bumper of the car up ahead of us on a westbound road, trudging about one mile an hour. My parents and I were returning from Maryland to California after World War II ended. It was obvious as we drove by that we would get to where we were going much sooner than he or his driver would get just about anywhere. We had the power, they had the dusty heat.

I identified with the donkey. As we passed, I said, "That's mean!" My parents had no response. Perhaps they were thinking about the duck hunting planned at their cousin's upcoming home on a lake. "That's mean" hung in the air and still sticks with me.

Some weeks later we were living in West Los Angeles. My only memory of that period was when my mother scolded me on a Saturday workday. She called down the stairs to me to say, "Allan, when you're dusting stairs, start at the top and work down, not at the bottom and work up." My own reaction was, "Nobody ever told me that." I felt judged by an invisible system: "This isn't fair." But I was not so quick to notice the injustice I inflicted on others.

One time I asked a girl down the street from our house in Pasadena to close her eyes so that, it turned out, I could hit her buttocks with a wooden fence slat. This betrayal of her trust soon had her mother calling my mother on the phone. Within less than half an hour I was ringing Violet's doorbell and offering a bouquet of flowers to convey regrets and to apologize for what I had done. I think I had to spend the rest of the day indoors in my mother's bedroom.

II. School Years

I struggled to survive in the public schools because I was so small and young in relation to my classmates. I started kindergarten when I was not yet five. On my first day of class I ran home crying, and didn't understand what was bothering me. I was so little and outside my usual social circle. I had the experience all through elementary and middle school of being the top student in the class academically, but isolated because I was socially immature.

I was an adventurous and foolish instigator looking for action. When I was about eleven, I pulled the seat from under the largest girl in my class just as she sat down. When she sprawled out on the floor all the boys in the class were laughing and the girls were outraged. Somehow I got away with that and the class went on.

When I caused a disturbance, I'd watch how my parents reacted. My dad would wait to see what my mom said because she had a year or two of teacher training on how to keep class discipline and what to expect of kids. Dad respected her on that. His approach was to say, "Dorothy is in charge until you're twelve, and after that, I'm in charge." My younger brother, sister, and I created a lot of fuss under mom's regime.

I was something of a noisy kid, talked a lot, interrupted a lot—rather self-centered. Then in middle school I began to attend Methodist summer camps, and would send home letters about my aspirations to become a better person. I remember our church membership class standing before the congregation and affirming basic Christian convictions. Guilt and shame were working in me to do better. I became vice president and president of our church sixty-person young adult fellowship. And during college, I attended the Wesleyan Foundation and contributed to its newsletter at Stanford.

III. Growing Up in the Post-World War II Era

I was something of an insecure kid who tried hard to be somebody. High achievement was a good way to gain recognition. I wasn't super athletic, but I could do outstandingly good work in the sciences, social sciences, or whatever the teachers put before me. I turned out to have a multi-directional attraction to learning. From middle school on, or even earlier, I wanted to achieve, I wanted to compete, I wanted to win. That was a big driving force in my character.

Another guidance system came from grandparents and other relatives in the Los Angeles area who thought I was an outstanding toddler with a great future. This was expressed in letters and pictures in an album that communicated their view that I had the material to become "president of the United States." In a post-war context filled with soldiers in uniform, parents were prone to idolize their older children as future war heroes or other notable celebrities. So during my childhood, I received more than my share of assurances that if I lived my life right I could end up in the White House.

In high school I went out for tennis, but within a couple of weeks I'd been demoted to the second team, and saw that I might fall even lower. So, I dropped out of that and concentrated on areas where I could win.

I had only five Bs in my high school years and ended up fifth in my large, high-achieving Arcadia High School graduating class. I was accepted to go to Stanford, which, at that time, did not have many students coming from public schools. Initially, I thought I might not be able to compete with private school guys. But my folks were upper-middle class who could afford to get me into the Experiment in International Living, which sent me to Europe for four months in the Black Forest and five weeks in Bavaria with a group of elite students. I had studied German in high school and learned the language proficiently while in Germany.

IV. Discovering a Radical Jesus and Pacifism

A good friend came back from summer camp having listened to a radical Methodist speaker talk about pacifism. When I heard him tell about the idea, I became interested in pacifism too. I wondered how to do what Jesus said about loving your enemies. My Dad had been in the Pentagon during World War II, procuring supplies for the military, and my uncle was an officer on subchasers and landing craft in the Pacific who was very lucky to survive. They argued with me, but they never actually wanted to talk about their war experiences. I had a ten-year argument with my folks about these kinds of things. Later, in 1987, I got a letter from my mom in which she wrote how deeply she had been impacted by the positions I took on race relations, peace, community, and related things.

Studying Dietrich Bonhoeffer's writings and life greatly influenced me. Few of his works had been translated into English at that time, but I could read primary sources in German, becoming something of an expert on him. I wrote my senior dissertation on his pacifism. I declared my conscientious objection to war in my junior year of college when I applied for that status to my draft board. Then, after graduation, I had a huge disagreement with my folks when I followed through and announced my plans to do alternative service in a poor, Black section of Chicago for $10 a month from 1963 to 1965.

V. Finding My People at Church of Hope

After graduating from Stanford in 1963, I drove cross-country with a couple of friends who dropped me off at the West Side Christian Parish (WSCP) for my two years of alternative to military service. At that time the WSCP consisted of four storefront churches. We volunteers lived at Project House—women on the third floor, and men on the first and second floors, to keep the women safe in this rough part of Chicago. We all ate dinners together and had important life-changing conversations. I was assigned to work with Church of Hope, where Julius Belser was the lead pastor, closely assisted by Peggy Belser and Hilda Carper. Julius had a considerable influence on me as a mentor—we both liked each other. At first I focused on community organizing work, but soon I became fascinated by the communal life at Church of Hope where educated Whites, single Black moms on welfare, and a few middle-class Blacks shared all things in common in the model of Acts 2.

It took me a year to really "get" what was happening in the church community. The startling thing for me was to see Black people be quite honest with White people despite educational and class differences in our small group setting. It wasn't easy going. One Black woman, Rose, walked out of our small group meeting two times in one evening because she couldn't stand being so close to White people. But then she came back to tell us her grief about her grandson being sent back to prison. I had never before experienced this level of trust and honest sharing between people. God was doing something real here. In the words of Julius Belser, we were not do-gooders "throwing pennies over the wall"; this was the nitty-gritty reconciliation that Jesus came to demonstrate which changes everyone, and I was hooked. God had directed my steps and helped me find my people. Now, fifty-five years later, Julius and Peggy, Hilda, Albert and Carol, Jeanne and I are still together in this same life. What bonds of love and loyalty we've been given! Though the Black members of the Church of Hope did not follow us to Reba when our neighborhood was bulldozed a few years later, grateful relationships with Rose and Rena remained until death intervened.

VI. Finding My Vocation as a Community Organizer

When I came to the West Side Christian Parish right out of college in 1963, I was tired of reading and writing about peace issues and going to conferences. As a registered conscientious objector to war, I was eager to get into the action. The others guys living at Project House of the West Side Christian Parish were interested in justice issues too, but were not organizers. Our daily service was to take area youth to activities, sporting events, field trips, etc. David Gale, another volunteer from Project House, and I pulled together the Parish Youth Action Committee (PYAC) made up of high school and post-high school kids who were free during the summer.

The Urban League did research into justice issues in Chicago, like overcrowded schools, discriminatory housing, swimming pools that refused Black kids, etc. PYAC would gather people for demonstrations, marches, and rallies for such causes. We'd train them in nonviolent direct action before sending them into a public witness. We kept at it for a couple of years and established an integrated (Blacks and Whites together) presence for justice on the Near West Side of Chicago.

Soon after PYAC got started we began organizing folks to go to the March on Washington (August 28, 1963), where Martin Luther King Jr. and others were going to speak. We got about eighteen youth and chaperones to go in a chartered bus, along with many other busses from Chicago. We drove all night, participated in the huge rally of two hundred thousand people, heard MLK Jr. give his "I Have a Dream" speech. Then we got back in our bus and rode home over the next night. That event created a huge impression on us all.

VII. Finding My Life Partner

I'd been in a couple of other serious relationships at Stanford, hoping to get married, but it turned out we did not have enough unity on matters of faith and how we would raise children. I didn't want to get into a situation in which I'm married to this person because I've fallen in love, but we don't have unity on these important things. Being in love helps stay together, but it is not enough. That's a word of wisdom I got from a high school youth pastor, and it stuck with me. A couple of women from Stanford visited me in Chicago, but when they saw the neighborhood I lived in, their interest faded away.

Jeanne and I were well aware of each other at Project House. She was the housemother, the financial manager, and the administrator of meals and hospitality. I was a leader among the men, so we had to deal with each other a good bit. Jeanne was a terrific looking woman in her twenties: people would give me nudges and say, "Look over there." But the "aha" moment for me was when Jeanne stated her desire to join Church of Hope—where I was also attending. Suddenly, I saw her as someone who shared my radical life commitments. For two years we had been formed in the Anabaptist understanding of church as community, so we already had most of the important issues in common. But her commitment to Church of Hope awakened a romantic interest for me because I could imagine a future together. I had developed a line in my mind I would not cross, that sexual relations were for after marriage. As Jeanne and I began serious dating, I said, "You know what? I think we should get married." And after about three seconds she said, "So do I."

Allan and Jeanne cutting their wedding cake, Christmas Day, 1965

Jeanne's folks had never visited her on the West Side. They thought that part of the city was so terrible. We got invited to their house and they liked me. I was used to making decisions without consulting my parents, but my folks liked Jeanne a lot too. So with our parents' permission, we got engaged around Halloween.

Jeanne was an English teacher at Crane High School, so she only had two weeks off at Christmas. We claimed one week to get ready for the wedding and one week for a honeymoon. Most of the people who were coming could be free on Christmas day, so that's when we got married, December 25, 1965.

VIII. Finding My Theologian

In 1965, after completing my two years of alternative to military service, I began to attend Chicago Theological Seminary on a Presidential Scholarship in order to study under the renowned Anabaptist scholar Franklin Littell.

During our time at the WSCP, we had a visit from a budding young theologian from Goshen, Indiana, named John Howard Yoder. We asked his advice about getting involved with a political campaign for alderman in our ward. We wanted to back Florence Scala: a reform-minded restaurant operator running against a corrupt incumbent named John D'Arco. John Howard Yoder asked us many astute questions and affirmed the validity of what we were doing since it aspired to nonviolent social change. However, he was more interested in the poor communal interracial Church of Hope, and helped us see more clearly that we were engaged in the new world order in line with Jesus and the early church, a radical alternative to the dominant Constantinian politic of history. I realized, "I have met my theologian."

As it turned out, our hopes for political change were dashed on election day. The D'Arco bosses would knock on people's doors in the projects. Anyone who wanted $5.00 could get a ride to vote against Scala, who ended up with only 30 percent of the vote. It was a bitter wake-up call for me to see how the powers and principalities of this world are entrenched against the forces of goodness, and how terrible were the political options in Chicago government.

In August 1966, we moved to Elkhart, Indiana, so I could study under John Howard Yoder at the Associated Mennonite Biblical Seminary (now the Anabaptist Mennonite Biblical Seminary). It was an exciting time as we were exposed to the radical ideas John Howard Yoder was working on that soon came out in his landmark book, *The Politics of Jesus*. We lived on campus and then moved to Benham Avenue to be near the Yoder family to explore intentional Christian community with them and with Marsha and Jerry Lind. Jeanne taught in the Elkhart High School before our son, Mark, was born in December 1967.

Life together brought our three families into close relationship, but the intentional community did not work out because J. H. Yoder was often gone to conferences and speaking engagements, unable to provide the presence and leadership our group needed.

IX. Joining Reba and the Charismatic Renewal

After my graduation at AMBS with a master's degree in 1969, Jeanne and I moved to Reba Place Fellowship so I could begin a doctoral program at Garrett Evangelical Seminary. We moved in at 836 Elmwood next door to the family of Julius and Peggy Belser, who had been our mentors back in the Church of Hope on the Near West Side of Chicago. The house church and community we'd all been part of on Peoria Street had disbanded because the neighborhood was bulldozed to make space for the new University of Illinois in Chicago campus. Most of the White folks from our community on Peoria Street also moved to Reba like Albert Steiner, David and Margaret Gale, Conrad and Martyne Wetzel, and Hilda Carper.

When Jeanne and I got married, we had not thought much about adoption, but after the birth of Mark we weren't conceiving again, and so we began to think about it. We learned that there were many interracial babies in foster care that the agencies struggled to find placements for. We went to Children's Home and Aide and found a social worker, Mrs. Parshall, who was impressed by our openness to interracial adoption and Reba's support system. Kathy came home with us in 1970, three months after her birth. She proved to be a quiet but observant kid. James Marcus came to us in 1971, at the age of five months. He was already very sociable and connected easily with others. In subsequent years, though community leadership issues were often challenging for us adults, our children have been explicitly grateful for their experiences, especially the long-term friends they made in extended-household life like Orwin and Sally Youngquist.

During this time the charismatic renewal was sweeping through many church and community groups as people experienced the baptism of the Holy Spirit, an outpouring of gifts, often the gifts of physical and emotional healing. We learned about this renewal firsthand when some of us visited the Church of the Redeemer in Houston, Texas, under the leadership of Graham Pulkingham. We came back convinced that their large, extended-family households could be the context for the rapid healing and spiritual growth of many otherwise struggling people. This was basically the same vision that Julius and Peggy Belser had already begun to live out at the Clearing Household at 722 Monroe.

I had studied Bonhoeffer and was familiar with his vision of community in *Life Together*. The household model was a way to do community in a more intensive way. After two years of classes at seminary with only my dissertation to complete, I became totally immersed in the charismatic renewal that brought many new folks to Reba for an all-out Christian life.

At this time Goshen College invited me to teach a Bible course, but I was convinced that God was doing something so vital and innovative at Reba, that this is where I should stay. It seemed timely that I finish my PhD work at Garrett Seminary. However, at this time four professors that I knew at Garrett got divorced from their wives, including my dissertation advisor. I felt betrayed. I was not impressed by the academic environment as a place where people's lives are transformed by what they were studying. Dietrich Bonhoeffer, on the other hand, left academia to found a discipleship training community that he wrote about in *Life Together*. For me, he was an exemplary hands-on counselor, teacher, and community leader. I felt like this guy has the theology and the practices that American theologians needed and that Reba was living out. We had come to Reba Place Fellowship, and that's why I happened to go to Garrett Seminary, not the other way around.

X. Unlearning the Need to Win

After folks got to know me better in community, Hilda Carper confronted me and asked, "Why do you always need to shade the truth in your own favor?" My competitive spirit was a deep habit that caused needless arguments. Others challenged me on my tendency to see myself over against others in community discussions. During the time of the charismatic renewal I felt convicted to take a retreat and ask God to take this contentious spirit from me. It has been a long struggle, but I've found much more joy in teamwork than in winning arguments. I've learned to peacefully listen and "take it to heart" whenever someone brings me a concern.

About that time, Virgil Vogt, a Reba elder, challenged me to accept Jesus as my personal savior. Otherwise, he explained, the ego will always be at the center of your life. That made sense to me and it had a big effect on my spiritual life. It was, you might say, my evangelical conversion.

XI. The Toad Hall Era (1972–1976)

Before the charismatic renewal movement came to Reba Place Fellowship we were about thirty adults. But after that our life was transformed in many ways—new music, more exuberant worship, and many new people coming to get in on what the Holy Spirit was doing. By 1978, at the peak of the positive growth process, we were 156 adult members living in a dozen extended-family households. The rapid growth was exciting for me. I was very grateful for all the childcare help we got because we were very overwhelmed with the care of three young kids.

Together, Jeanne and I began the second Reba household at 714 Monroe with a bunch of energetic young people. They pitched right in on the childcare and the chores, and generally did a good job. We named the household Toad Hall after a scene in *The Wind in the Willows* by Kenneth Graham, which many of us were reading. It was a fun household with a lot of joking around, and with rather loose supervision. Many needy people came to the Clearing Household, and when they got full, Julius Belser would send them our way. Rather quickly we grew from seven to twenty people tucked into every possible space. And then some single men down the street were added to our dinner table. The place was hopping. In the basement there was a coffee house open one evening a week with an open mike for folk musicians and other hippie types. It was a cool anti-establishment hang-out for many Northwestern students. Sally Schreiner (now Youngquist) came to Reba by that route. A sample of the optimistic spirit of the place might be conveyed in the story of a fishing trip that almost happened.

One weekend I invited the five-to-ten-year-old boys at Reba along with their friends to come on a fishing trip to the Illinois River. We got about eight participants with me driving the van. All went well except for the weather and the equipment. By the time we got to the campsite the weather had changed from a light drizzle to an average rainstorm. We worked together on our tent and camping gear, but we were unable to find the tent pegs. I took responsibility for not getting them packed and explained how the right size and strength of twigs could be found in the woods if we worked together. Everyone worked on that vision until we had our big tent set up. Some of us wanted to sleep in our van and others wanted to sleep in the tent close by. I approved that arrangement before we divided up our two sleeping teams.

Several hours later, in pitch darkness, I was awakened by complaints. With the storm unrelenting the tent had fallen down on its campers. We decided that it would be better to go home rather than live out the storm in misery for the entire night. So our team worked together to shake the water off the tent and "pack" it into the back of our van. I did the driving and found the way back to Evanston clear and easy without any rush hour traffic, roughly two to three hours after midnight.

I maintained an optimistic spirit throughout this whole mini-disaster and overall felt we had done what we could with the bad weather and bad planning that undermined this particular camping and fishing trip. Spirits were high or exhausted depending on whom you asked. As an inexperienced leader, I was good at ignoring the warning signs and focusing instead on the good news in every situation.

XII. The Collapse of Toad Hall and the Reba Review

A lot of good things were happening at Toad Hall: a general experience of solidarity, respect for one another, and amazingly transparent conversation. We also made a lot of mistakes in that period. I was overloaded—finishing up graduate school, leading a household with Jeanne, attending leadership meetings, and overseeing individuals with pastoral care. I was doing all this social engineering to try and restructure the design and lines of authority and growth patterns of people in community. I was doing a lot of troubleshooting. I was not attentive enough to what Jeanne was experiencing at home with small children and too much responsibility. She complained to the elders, who immediately jumped on the problem, which was me being overextended.

Toad Hall household: Allan on the stair railing to the left, Jeanne on the left of the top row, and Hilda Carper laughing in the middle.

There was a spectrum of leadership styles at Reba with Julius and me on the more relaxed and relational end, and John Lehman on the more authoritarian end. After Jeanne's "resignation," we came under the supervision of John Lehman, who shut down Toad Hall and brought in Russ and Pat Harris to lead in our place. For a couple of years Jeanne and I lived in something of an internal exile in the same household, though it was no longer called Toad Hall. A lot of dissatisfaction was focused on me. I did not want to fight with Jeanne, so I went along with the discipline.

It was discerned that I needed to focus more on my marriage and family, and to get more practical rather than academic experience, so I worked as a social worker from 1972 to 1976 with Travelers and Immigrants Aid in Union Station dealing with travelers in crisis. Then I took up my dissertation work again, graduating in 1978.

We stayed on through this heavy season because we felt called to the life and the relationships in general. We stayed because of our loyalty and long-term relationship to Julius, Peggy, and Hilda. Our kids were thriving and not suffering in household life. And where could we go with an interracial family? At that point society in general was very segregated, but this neighborhood was multi-racial.

By the end of the seventies, there was a season of general review at Reba when many people came forward with complaints of heavy-handed and arbitrary authoritarian moves on the part of the leadership. The elders listened and made sincere apologies, which made the whole community experience more credible for us. You can read all about that in Dave Jackson's book *Glimpses of Glory*. At the end of the review, most of the other households were disbanded and people returned to a more decompressed way of life in family-based living units. Reba Place Church was established with two kinds of membership—congregational and communal, which is where we remained. Other households (the Clearing, for example) continued but with more care, humility, practicing confession and forgiveness. Through all the changes, the charismatic movement at Reba Place continued to provide a helpful new participation in the active and living presence of the Holy Spirit.

XIII. Household Life at 723 Seward

In 1978, I completed my dissertation and graduated with a PhD from Northwestern University in biblical studies. That same year, Jeanne and I launched a new, more modest household at 723 Seward. We finished out the third floor to add a fifth bedroom, making more space for hospitality. And there we lived in relative peace for thirty-four years—thirty of those years were with Linda Kelsey, while others came and went. Others who lived with us for shorter periods of time were Bob and Martha Pennebaker, Susanne Coalson and Elspeth, Lois Engelman, Chris Evans with Karl, Dave Johnson, Brian Mosher, Bjorn Oda, Donald Berry, Brent Styan, Conrad Wetzel, Matthew Williams, and several other Reba interns. By this time we were wiser and knew our own limits. Rather than have people sent to us, we were inviting the people ourselves. We have hosted small group suppers of up to eighteen people at our long table. Jeanne is a good cook and host who knows how to put lots of food on for guests. We enjoy table conversation with young people especially.

Jeanne and Allan with children Mark, James Marcus, and Kathleen, ca. 1986

The story of Linda's arrival and integration into our family is worth telling. We first got to know Linda in the seventies when she was a student at Wheaton College researching a paper on Christian intentional community living. After graduation she showed up at our door, saying she'd rented an apartment nearby. She had landed in a dangerous neighborhood north of Howard on Callan in Evanston, was studying at the University of Chicago in social work, and working at Giordano's Pizza. Jeanne invited her to live with us where the rent was much cheaper and the neighborhood safer. In a few weeks she moved in and stayed—a wonderful fit. Linda's parents were missionaries in Jordan so she adopted us as her second home. She became like our oldest child and a thirty-year partner in anchoring the household life as others came and went. She has been responsible, loyal, good for our children, always eager to help—a God-sent angel. All this time she has been a social worker in some of Chicago's more challenging schools. To this day she brings a salmon take-out dinner once a week to share with us and our guests.

XIV. North Suburban Peace Initiative

Once my dissertation was done, I had time to become more involved in the peace movement. My part-time efforts grew when participating churches, especially a UCC congregation in Wilmette, made serious financial commitments so that we could found the North Suburban Peace Initiative, of which I was named the founding director. The primary threat to human survival at that time was the nuclear arms race between the U.S. and the Soviet Union. During the ten years of my leadership we organized delegations to connect with peace movements in the Soviet Union and other countries. We added our strength to the Nuclear Freeze campaign. Each year we hosted fundraising events for NSPI, bringing in top-name speakers from around the world. The NSPI office was in our basement, where Jeanne joined me as bookkeeper for the organization. We hosted many mailing parties at our large dining room table, so our home became the peace movement center for the North Shore from '78 to '88. Beyond that we remained active in the movement and could celebrate with others the fall of the Berlin Wall in '89 and the collapse of the Soviet Union in '91.

XV. Working for Illinois Mennonite Conference in Chicago

After my service to the North Shore Peace Initiative, I wanted to be more involved in pastoral work. In 1991 I was invited to join the Illinois Mennonite Mission Commission with responsibility to support the Chicago area Mennonite Churches. Many of them were minority ethnic congregations stuck in difficult leadership transitions. By taking time to come alongside, I was trusted enough to help mediate some conflicts and straighten out some administrative breakdowns.

Also, for more than two decades, I served as chairman of the board for Reba Place Early Learning Center—a child-care center that Hilda Carper begin in a Reba Fellowship living room, and which grew over time to involve a dozen teachers caring for fifty preschool children. We were always near the edge of financial failure, but a network of friends emerged to save it and help it grow for another day. Now RELC is one of the best early learning centers in the area, standing on its own feet as a nonprofit with funding help from the City of Evanston United Way. The NSPI and RELC put me in touch with many of the best people on the Chicago North Shore as a community organizer.

XVI. Leadership at Reba

Then, beginning in 2003, I was elected Reba Place Fellowship Leader for two three-year terms. During that time, I gave a lot of attention to understanding and reorganizing the administrative structures of the Fellowship, and bringing the members along so that we could reform and unify our scattered operations. I had to work closely with David Johnson, our master bookkeeper, to do this. We ended up closing down the Rogers Park property management office and bringing everything under one accounting system so that our year-end reports could be reconciled for tax purposes and for the clearer understanding of Fellowship members.

During this time, the Fellowship purchased a mini-mall at Pratt and Ashland in the Rogers Park neighborhood of Chicago for $1,000,000 to provide a home for the Living Water Community Church. The Fellowship could buy the building quickly, and then, over time, sell it to the church. That gave the congregation a home and a strong presence in a troubled neighborhood where other Fellowship members already lived.

Then we purchased the very run-down 1528 Pratt apartment building with fifty-one small units affordable to immigrants and others one step above homelessness. We knew the $3,000,000 building had many problems to tackle, but we had not counted on digging up all the bottom floor units to replace the plumbing and heating lines—which cost half a million more than we'd budgeted for. This put a strain on the whole RPF housing system, but by spreading out the costs, we got through.

About that time the housing market crashed, so the value of all our property fell. But this also gave me the opportunity to consolidate all our mortgages at lower interest rates so that we could pay our loans off faster. Though property values fell this did not bother us because the need for affordable rental units remained strong. Now the 1528 Pratt building is a huge asset to the neighborhood and to the Living Water Church Community Church because many members can live in proximity and build community with each other in a safe, decent, and affordable environment.

After Sally Schreiner Youngquist took over leadership of the Fellowship in 2009, I continued as the Administrator on the RPF Leadership Team while she focused on other areas. We've made a good team on the Leadership Committee. Sally has been such a gifted leader, teacher, exhorter, senior care giver—we aren't going to do better than that. She is amazing in all she can do so efficiently. People really trust and appreciate her.

XVII. Our Family: James Marcus's Death

I've been on the phone regularly with Mark and Kathy. While James Marcus was a carefree, adventurous guy, his older brother Mark took a more traditional route of college, marriage, law school, and a career in Green Bay, Wisconsin, as a defense attorney. Mark and Judy have raised two fine girls who now are young adults and doing well academically. Mark has made some personal trips to care for me now that I suffer from Lewy body disease.

Kathy was very shy at first and said little until she was nine years old. I'm amazed at how she became a successful teacher, union representative, and mother—a very good and responsible adult. We've had a phone date every Friday morning. She is doing a good job of raising a family with her lesbian partner in Seattle.

Over the years, when our kids came to visit, we'd turn the living room into a guest room and do all we could together for a few days, visiting museums, parks, and zoos in Chicago with our grandchildren.

For the last six years or so of James Marcus's life, he would call me about once a week and ask for fatherly advice about matters of marriage, family, career, and faith. Earlier, he tried to break into acting as a career. Though he felt a lot of satisfaction in it, his successes were few. Eventually he worked his way up the ladder in video and movie production until, in 2012, he became a member of the Director's Guild of America.

He had always been someone who prayed, but in his later years he found some other Christian African Americans in this profession and identified publicly as a Christian. Marcus and Danae asked me to officiate at their wedding, which happened on a chartered boat on the Puget Sound outside Seattle.

My mind goes numb and my memory blanks out when I try to think about how the news came to us of James Marcus's sudden and violent death. Here is how Sandy Banks tells that story in the *Los Angeles Times* (December 23, 2013).

> James Marcus Howe was shot to death on his front porch in a tussle with thugs trying to force their way into his home the day before Thanksgiving. His wife was wounded and hospitalized, his young son was traumatized.
>
> The Howe [parents] learned of his death from their daughter-in-law, who called from the hospital. She said, "Mommy Jeanne,

are you sitting down? . . . Someone came to the door and rang the bell." She said that she had been shot and that Marcus had died.[1]

The article goes on to describe the funeral, where four hundred friends, relatives, and coworkers showed up with testimonies of Marcus's generosity and unfailing good cheer. The article concludes with Jeanne and Allan's astonishing perspective of forgiveness and hope for the redemption of their son's killers.

> "When Jesus says 'love your enemies, do good to those who hurt you' . . . we take that pretty seriously," said Allan.
>
> "I'm sorry the people who killed my son couldn't know what they were doing," Jeanne said. "If they had known him and he had known them, he would have won their hearts, he was such an outgoing person."

There was a second memorial service for James Marcus at Reba a few weeks after the first one in Los Angeles. Again, Jeanne and I were astonished by the outpouring of memories that recalled James Marcus's growing up years at Reba, his ability to animate good times for everyone in the place. It was good to feel close again and thank God for his life with all who knew him.

Jeanne and I went to a therapist for half a year after James Marcus's death. Jeanne had a lot more to talk about than I did. I tend to process things more intellectually and maybe not as profoundly. We still have times of sudden sadness that come over us when we think of the loss of our youngest son. But God is good and has given us many good things to be about, to live on with hope.

XVIII. Looking Back and Looking Forward

In 2013, after Jeanne had a fall, we realized it was time to move out of 723 Seward, a large house with too many stairs. So we sorted out a lot of stuff and moved to our "retirement home" in a first floor apartment at 737 Reba Place, right above Jeanne's desk at the Reba Services basement office.

Going through my file drawers has been a reminder of how I've spent my years. When people have asked me *how* I'm doing, I've often talked about *what* I'm doing instead. Now I treasure more just hanging out with

---

1. Sandy Banks, "True Christmas Spirit, from a Slain Man's Grieving Parents" (*Los Angeles Times*, December 23, 2013).

people to enjoy their company. Overall, I'm grateful for living and serving alongside Jeanne all these years. God couldn't have given me a better partner. My gifts have been well used. Most of the hard edges of my youthful self-centeredness have been knocked off by the friction and learning from years in community.

Allan Howe, taking the long view

A generation ago my father died of Alzheimer's disease. His decline was seven hard years. One time I found my father lost in a shopping mall and I cried inwardly, "Who stole my Dad?" Now something like this is happening to me. The doctor calls it Lewy body disease—something like Alzheimer's and Parkinson's together. In the last year, I've withdrawn from all the Reba committees and task teams I've served on. Adam Vaughan has taken over as community administrator. I have to trust others to carry on, which is sometimes hard for me. I've spent hours going through my papers and throwing things away or passing them on to others. I often need help. I like to bring projects to completion, but now I feel blocked from finishing what I begin. I experience a succession of broken-off thoughts. I can't find my words. I'm very grateful that you (David) are writing this down and making sense of it.

Allan and Jeanne in Allan's last weeks

Jeanne and I take walks to the lake, to Trader Joe's, to various parks. Sometimes I experience violent things that others tell me are delusions. This leaves me confused. I'm declining. But I feel like God is coming to my rescue, and this is my hope for what is to come.

(The following poem is added at Jeanne Howe's suggestion.)

The Lantern out of Doors

Sometimes a lantern moves along the night.
    That interests our eyes. And who goes there?
    I think; where from and bound, I wonder, where,
With, all down darkness wide, his wading light?

Allan Howe

Men go by me, whom either beauty bright
    In mould or mind or what not else makes rare:
    They rain against our much-thick and marsh air
Rich beams, till death or distance buys them quite.

Death or distance soon consumes them; wind,
    What most I may eye after, be in at the end
I cannot, and out of sight is out of mind.

Christ minds: Christ's interest, what to avow or amend
    There, eyes them, heart wants, care haunts, foot follows kind,
Their ransom, their rescue, and first, fast, last friend.

    —Gerard Manley Hopkins (1844–1889)

Seeing the Vision Through

Josh McCallister

We were a young and ambitious family eager to try on intentional community, paying a visit to Reba Place Fellowship in the spring of 2008. Allan Howe was our energetic tour guide through the web of backyards, basements, tight passageways between brick buildings, and living rooms where people were carrying on as usual despite the strangers being walked through. That cool April morning, Allan was so delighted with all the systems and productivity of the community it seemed as though Reba was just beginning. He had an appreciative spring in his step and a bright enthusiasm that betrayed his white hair.

Not many months later we arrived in a heavy rainstorm, unable to unload our rented moving van. Jeanne and Allan provided a place to stay and shared meals with us on Seward Street that evening. On the following day with pep and stamina, Allan worked with fifteen or twenty others to get our stuff up three flights of stairs, into our snug new home. Allan was the community leader at RPF during this story. A servant; a minister.

Allan and Jeanne became surrogate grandparents for our family in the five and a half years we spent at Reba Place Fellowship. First, we had one, then two, then three children eating and praying and discussing around the Howe table every week. Additionally, we belonged to a discipleship small group with the Howes for the same five years, meeting weekly. As it goes with intentional community, Allan and I were together on a number of committees, task teams, common work, and other such shared projects. We have celebrated many birthdays. Jeanne and Allan danced with us and our children during our covenant celebration when Candace and I joined the Fellowship. Jeanne called me the day she learned of the murder of their son, James Marcus. I think I know Allan well. It is a privilege to reflect to you what great impact Allan's friendship has given me.

Mr. Howe has kept his hand to the plow, working on his individual discipleship while also pursuing peace and justice in the world. His context in a specific tradition (Anabaptist) and in a specific location (Evanston) among a distinct community (RPF) over many decades is one outstanding witness Allan contributes to the world. By reading his memoir, you have learned of Allan's belief in Jesus and his decision to *believe what Jesus believed* about social change through nonviolent methods. These decisions happened in his youth, but they were carefully weighed at the time and then committed to in deeper and more costly ways as time wore on. As Nietzsche said it, "There should be long obedience in the same direction... something that has made life worth living."

One characteristic, one way of being in the world for Allan, is as an encourager. I've received a great deal of encouragement from Allan. He is a watchful leader, attentive to the people he has gathered around the table. A story comes to mind: a pair of young women from North Park University who were attending our potluck for a season. These two announced some business intentions that were youthful and uninformed. Allan patiently asked the type of business questions you might get from a loan manager at the bank. It became clear that the young women were not ready to open shop, but Allan's way was sincere and hopeful. I believe the students were challenged and empowered. They were certainly not put down; Allan was careful to keep their dream alive.

Being in a small group with the Howes, we shared many of our difficulties in marriage or with raising small children. Allan would affirm us as parents and pray for our discernment and strength to walk the path God has revealed to us.

When we announced our ambitious hopes for ministry, RPF led us through a process of group discernment in order to reach consensus. I remember a lot of meetings with different groups from the community. Sometimes the meetings were with folks who didn't know us well, and they had hard questions. Through all of that process, Allan was one of our encouragers. His questions were perceptive and important, but never did I feel he was trying to challenge my readiness. He assumed the best of my intentions, as did Jeanne. After we were sent out from Reba to pursue community in Little Rock, Arkansas, Allan remained on our support team for several years keeping our struggle in his prayers. Now that his health is failing, we do not connect on the phone as often as we used to, and I miss him.

Both during and after living in community with Allan, I have come to think more on the counter-cultural labor of commitment. Allan's concluding thoughts in the memoir speak to his intent to "see things through." I admire this quality in people, most especially in leaders. Rather than casting a vision and hoping workers will follow up on the tasks laid out, Allan wants to work out the problems and finish the job.

He once told me about a time when he'd damaged a van during the Church of Hope days. At that time Allan was a young man, less familiar with responsibility. Julius Belser informed him that they would be repairing the damage themselves, together, and Allan was surprised by that. The job required ingenuity and follow-through. I suppose this vignette is one of hundreds of other small lessons that were received in community. Julius was discipling Allan in his twenties to be the man who would face problems with hope and fortitude.

Finally, Allan was full of hope. While Allan was RPF leader he gathered support and attempted to open a retail business selling Amish furniture on Main Street. As I am told, the store had low traffic for many months in the opening, and members wanted to let it go, counting the endeavor as a loss. But Allan went on, working at the store and keeping the Fellowship in sync as business slowly built. I came into the life of Reba several years after Plain and Simple Amish Furniture was opened and I was invited to work there. Almost immediately after being hired, the economy crashed (fall of 2008). Through that cold hard winter and the next year, Allan was an engine of hope with a longer perspective than most of us. Our store survived and outlasted several competitors. Now Plain and Simple provides several jobs and regular support to the financial needs of Reba Place Fellowship. Allan taught us how to see the vision through.

~

Josh McCallister with his wife, Candace, and their three children, live in Little Rock, Arkansas, where Josh teaches grade school art. They are pursuing the formation of an intentional Christian community with other seekers.

A Lifetime of Making Straight Paths

GREG CLARK

You would not notice him at first. Allan Howe looks like hundreds of others in this winter of polar vortices and record snowfalls. With each step, the snow squeaks under his boots, *curchunk, curchunk*. He moves down the sidewalk, shoulders slightly hunched over, pushing his shovel like a plow. In the Chicago metro area, Allan is one of thousands of people shoveling their walks.

Allan was born in Washington, DC, in 1942, while his father was working in the Pentagon. After the war, Allan's family moved to Southern California, and his father earned a small fortune in the citrus industry. Allan went to Stanford; he graduated in 1963.

In the early 1960s, the war in Vietnam was still ramping up. In this context, making sense of right and wrong was not merely academic. So, while still a college student at Stanford, Allan took a retreat for the purpose of reading through the Gospels. There he found a God who reestablishes community with us and with all creation, while we were still God's enemies. Allan concluded that one could not both follow Jesus and advocate violent solutions to problems—not the problems of the world, not of the country, not of a family, not of an individual.

If Allan's realization had remained only theoretical, it would have made no difference. But when Allan started to act on this realization, to order his life to practice nonviolence, he began to pay a price. He filed for and received conscientious objector status. This was no small thing for a young man raised in family with a strong military tradition, whose grandpa had him pegged to become president of the United States. He knew his own family would misunderstand him.

So, Allan gave up family, and houses, and fields. He became a bird without a nest. As a conscientious objector, Allan began his "alternative service" in June of 1963. His alternate service landed him in a small church in Chicago. Here he discovered a radically different community. The church was intergenerational, interracial, and, because it focused on living with the poor, it cut across socioeconomic boundaries. Church members shared meals, money, and living quarters. They shared daily conversation about life's joys, its pains, and the experience of aching need. From expressions of need came a realignment of resources. The common table was the basis for a common purse. This church was the tree in which many birds of the air found their nests.

Soon after Allan arrived, he was given the job of organizing a bus trip for African-American teens to join the March on Washington. It was a heady start in dizzying times, but it was also what needed to be done.

In January, winter rolled in, and Allan found what it meant to trade pleasant winters of Pasadena for the winter winds of the Midwest. With the same determination with which he organized the bus trip in August, he set himself to clearing the sidewalks of snow. It was what needed to be done.

In 1965, Allan had fulfilled his commitment of two years of alternative service in Chicago. He could have gone back to California and reentered a life oriented toward the pursuit of money and prestige. Instead, he chose to stay. Something had taken root in him, and his life grew. He went on to graduate school, and in 1978 he completed a PhD in New Testament. He had offers to make a career as a professor. Again, he needed to choose. But how?

By this time, Allan had been living in community fifteen years, and he had learned to ask a different set of questions. Practices like sharing food, shelter, and money, and practices like reconciling with your enemy teach their practitioners that God can show up anywhere and in anyone. If God is at work in Jesus, and if that work reconciles God and the world, where did he find that happening?

Allan and his wife, Jeanne, did not simply decide by themselves; the community came around them to help discern. But in the end, the decision was still their own. Here is how Allan still assesses the situation thirty-five years later: "The world has an awful lot of New Testament professors. I think what the world really needs is more Christian communities that take the life and teaching of Jesus seriously."

Allan gave up possible careers in the military, in business, and in the academy to be part of a small planting. The Stanford Cardinal is not going to put him on their website to advertise what you can do with a Stanford education. But you would have the wrong idea if you think his choices were costly, depressing, and unfulfilling. On the contrary, Allan has gained more than he ever gave up. Allan helped found and led the North Suburban Peace Initiative. He has started numerous businesses, both for-profit and not-for-profit. He sits on several boards of directors and has mentored younger entrepreneurs. He's been to Russia and El Salvador on peacemaking missions. He draws on his academic training regularly to teach classes. Most important, he has been son, and brother, and father to hundreds of people.

Now, after fifty winters, Allan still shovels the snow. When the blizzards come, he pulls on his boots, takes hold of his shovel, and makes straight paths. Allan does not just shovel the walk in front of his own house. He walks around the entire block shoveling snow, and then moves on to the next block, and the next. He shovels the walks that connect everyone who lives in community. For people just making their way to their jobs, Allan's lifelong selfless labor does not come into focus. But there is a cardinal in the branches overhead who sees, and he announces God's good pleasure: "Cheer! Cheer! Cheer!"

This is an excerpt from a larger talk given March 28, 2014, at Trinity Christian College chapel by Greg Clark, Reba Fellowship member and philosophy professor at North Park University.

Through the Needle's Eye

David Janzen

As we gather to remember our friend, Allan Howe, I want to reflect with you why I'm not feeling sad, but joyful about how heaven came to earth in Allan's life.

In 1984 our family moved to Reba Place Fellowship, and landed just across the street from the Howes who lived at 723 Seward. Our children were the same age, and often played together. Allan and I were peers in many ways, so for thirty-five years we have mentored each other. Each Wednesday noon I'd carry my lunch plate across the street and sit down with Allan to eat, talk, and pray about everything on our minds. In recent years our meeting place moved a block north, to Allan and Jeanne's retirement apartment at 737 Reba Place. Over the years of our meetings, Allan was always cheerful company. There was a sweetness and easiness about our conversation that could wander freely into any topic on our minds, any community issue, or any learning for which we wanted to give thanks. Often, we'd read from our journals and try to discern what God was doing in our lives.

Allan had a quick wit. A sneaky smile could spread across his face as he'd think of some ironic connection his agile mind had made. We enjoyed the joke about the privileged White male who was born on third base and went through life believing he'd hit a triple.

If you get a chance to read Allan's memoir, you'll see that he grew up in wealth and privilege, in a White neighborhood in Arcadia, California, where their family had a wide, ranch-style house under palm trees, surrounded by flower gardens and with a swimming pool in the back. Allan's grandpa used to brag that this smart grandson of his would one day become president of the United States. But somewhere in his youth Allan heard about pacifism and Christian community. While an honors student at Stanford University, Allan studied the Gospels and read Bonhoeffer to determine if this was, indeed, what Jesus taught and what the early church practiced. And with that revelation, he set out on a path to rediscover the life of Jesus with fellow disciples and the poor.

In the Gospels we read about a rich young ruler who came to Jesus and asked the sincere question, "What must I do to inherit eternal life?" Jesus challenged him and said, "If you want to go all the way with that question, sell what you have, give it to the poor, and come follow me." The rich young man went away sorrowfully because he had many possessions. Jesus observed, "It is easier for a camel to go through the eye of a needle than for a rich man to enter heaven." "But with God," Jesus adds, "all things are possible." God used the circumstances of Allan's life to show how a rich man can pass through the eye of a needle and enter the kingdom of heaven. A naked and humble soul can pass through the eye of the needle, but his possessions cannot. Allan spent his life giving away his material, intellectual, and spiritual possessions, and found daily joy in the company of the poor and other friends that Jesus gave him in community.

So, in our weekly conversations, Allan and I found companionship in scheming how to give away the gifts that God had given us, and thus bring heaven to earth. It was hard work, and it was easy. It was wrenching and it was joyful. It was a real and intimate life.

And then, as Allan declined in recent months, and his sleep patterns became more unpredictable, eating together on Wednesday noons no longer worked. I'd show up in the afternoon to give Jeanne a break. And if Alan was awake, we might take a walk or look at pictures if that's what he wanted to do. One time we walked to our apartment and watched an historical video of the Austrian city of Hallstat. Allan cried through much of the hour, but he wanted to keep watching. At the end, he thanked me from the heart. As his dementia increased the size of his world kept decreasing. It seems to me this shrinking world is what he might have been grieving.

In many ways the last two years of Allan's journey were another kind of giving away, of pruning everything as his mind, health, his natural optimism and ability to care for himself were gradually stripped away. But still, he was surrounded by love, the love of Jeanne, his friends, his helpers, and of God who was always near in prayer.

Allan's memoir concludes with this observation from last December: "Jeanne and I take walks to the lake, to Trader Joe's, to various parks. Sometimes I experience violent things that others tell me are delusions. This leaves me confused. I'm declining. But I feel like God is coming to my rescue, and this is my hope for what is to come."

In recent months I've lost a father figure in Julius Belser, someone as close as a son in Adrian Willoughby, and now my best friend, Allan Howe. But I'm not sad. The conversation we've had for thirty-five years goes on because we are connected in Jesus. The way we talked with each other then, is the way we still talk with Jesus now. There is freedom to tell Jesus whatever comes to mind. There we find that nothing that can separate us from his love. That conversation is a bridge between eternity and time. It is the way heaven comes to earth, and earth comes to heaven. In that way, our brother Allan, who has left us gradually over the past couple of years, is still with us because he is in Jesus and Jesus is in us, and the conversation never has to end. Passing through the needle's eye, Allan reminds us that only what is given away in love remains. And that makes me glad.

(Notes from David Janzen's sharing at Allan Howe's memorial service, Reba Place Church, July 13, 2019.)

SEVEN
Jeanne Casner Howe

How the March on Selma Moved One Sister to Leave Curlers behind and Become a Grateful, Lifelong, Simple-Life Servant of Jesus in Community

I. GROWING UP A WAIF

Though I always had a home, my younger sister and I grew up in a very lonely setting, often feeling neglected and abandoned. At the time I thought this was typical family life. Later on I learned how dysfunctional our family had been and I longed for other role models who could show me how to be a good wife and mother. My father often worked two jobs in downtown Chicago and returned to our far South Side home at 10:00 p.m. My mother was often gone from the house and we did not know why.

I remember coming home from kindergarten and waiting in our six-flat lobby till someone would let me in so I could play on the steps until mother came home. Sometimes neighbors would invite me in and give me supper. In the evenings, rather than cook, Mother would often send me out into the dark to a delicatessen to shop for food she wanted. I was never harmed, but now I feel unsafe thinking about it.

In middle school my mother worked downtown in a department store. I would come home from school with my younger sister (by then I had a key) and find a note instructing me to go buy pork chops or other food and make supper for my sister and me. I grew up lonely but thought this was normal.

My mother's life was quite disorganized. Often she would sleep late in the morning and wake up at the last minute when we had to rush off to school. My little sister would cry running after me, but I would leave her behind because I was afraid of getting a tardy mark at school.

My father would take me to Sunday school at a local church, but never attended himself. As a family we went to church on Christmas, Easter, Thanksgiving, and occasionally in the summer with my grandmother. During the summer I spent several weeks with my mother's family in St. Anne, Illinois. Though my grandmother never directly taught me about the faith, she was kind and stable, a pillar in an extended family with much mental illness. She could see that my mother was needy, and welcomed me into her home. I learned from her what a Christian is like.

Growing up, the only person of color I knew was Fanny Smith, who came to our apartment twice a month to do our laundry and ironing. The washing and drying machines were in the basement of our six-flat and we lived on the third floor. Fanny had to use the wooden back steps because Black people weren't allowed in the front hall in the 1940s and 1950s.

Over time I formed a bond with Fanny, who taught me how to iron. She took time to talk with me about many things. She was a solid Christian. Riding the Rock Island train to the Loop, I always tried to sit on the east side so that when we passed Sixty-Third Street I could see the Robert Taylor Homes under construction, and the rickety buildings nearby where Fanny lived. I'd think about the suffering that went with being poor and Black in Chicago.

When I was fourteen, my parents moved to a more upscale neighborhood and I began my sophomore year at a new school, Morgan Park. I didn't know anyone there, but a neighbor girl reached out to me and got me into a high school sorority, which was key to having a social life. At this time our school was one of the first to be integrated. Many Whites fled the neighborhood. But because I had been loved by Fanny Smith I felt comfortable and liked it there. I made friends and was elected to the student council my senior year. Dating was a big deal; some girls got pregnant and dropped out of school. I got serious about my studies and dropped out of the dating scene, which was a huge relief. The lives of two Christians, my grandma and Fanny Smith, gave me confidence to choose a different path.

II. College Years: Aspiring to a More Upscale Life

I'd been in a few plays in high school, so I wanted to go to college to major in theater. I applied to Illinois Wesleyan and got a half-tuition scholarship in drama. I also got into the Kappa Kappa Gama sorority as my mother had before me. My mother grew up in the Depression, and for her, having money was very important. She always wanted me to become well-to-do and she thought getting into a sorority was essential to that dream.

I played lead roles in a couple of Tennessee Williams plays. My method was to "be" that character all the time in whatever I did—eating, talking, walking, and so on. That way I did not have to "act" when I was on stage.

After two years I wanted to transfer to University of Illinois in Champaign; however, I was told I'd have to pay back my scholarship if I left, so I stayed at Wesleyan and became an English major. My mother was disappointed in my choice and cut off financial support. I thought I would have to drop out of school and earn money for a few years to complete my education. However, I had some unexpected allies. In my sophomore year I had a part-time job reading to an English professor who had weakened eyesight. When she heard I would have to drop out of school, she talked to the dean of the college who arranged for me to get free room and board in exchange for working in the dining hall for the majority of students. Ironically, my mother's decision to cut off my support forced me to make friends with people my mother would never have approved of: bright students from working-class backgrounds at Wesleyan on scholarships. They were an amazing group and changed my life.

During summers, I worked in the Loop as an elevator operator and a salesperson. I knew what it was like to be on my own with little parental support, which is why I could identify more easily with Blacks and other minorities. My senior year, Kappa Kappa Gamma elected me vice president so I could have free room and return to live at the sorority house, but I kept up with my new group of faithful friends.

In the English Department I had a few great professors who inspired me to read and appreciate writers like Gerard Manley Hopkins, who became my favorite poet. I was included in a selective class of about fifteen students with Joseph Meyers, a creative writing professor who had been a Jesuit novice before leaving the order and getting married. We met for two hours twice a week. We were Black, White, and other races. Professor Meyers would read our writing assignments aloud in class, so we got to know each other intimately across racial lines—something unknown in those days. In this group of brilliant, working-class students from many different backgrounds, race didn't matter, and we bonded deeply.

Oliver Jackson, a Black student on scholarship, and Gail Pitches, my best friend who was White, began living together. When Gail got pregnant, her parents wanted her to get an abortion. And when she married Oliver, her parents disowned her. Gail dropped out of school and moved with Oliver to St. Louis to live with his family where they had a son. The Jacksons's welcome of Gail in her desperate condition made a huge impression on me.

After graduation I was offered a job and taught three years in the Bloomington High School where I had done my practice teaching. However, I could not get a raise, I learned, unless I got a master's degree. So at the age of twenty-seven, I was living back home with my parents in Beverly, so I could afford graduate school at the University of Chicago. But my presence at home was causing problems, and I knew I should leave. I thought of my friend who had worked at the West Side Christian Parish and decided to call her to see if I could work there for the summer. Eventually I was approved as a summer volunteer with free room and board and a modest stipend.

III. I Discover My Spiritual Family: Project House and Church of Hope

Jeanne Casner is teaching Sunday School at Church of Hope

I moved to Project House on Fifteenth Street, about two blocks west of Ashland Avenue. This was an incredible coincidence because all the streets

I was most familiar with on the South Side were here—Laflin, Bishop, Loomis—but in a totally different mode. Not bungalows, two-flats, three-flats, and six-flats like where I was from, but rickety wooden buildings, and new high-rise projects with broken elevators. Still, in a strange way I had found a home where Fanny's world and my world came together—no longer pushed apart by racial segregation, but now united. I felt a joy and a deep peace. Now Chicago was together in my heart.

After two months at Project House I knew I wanted to stay, so when I got called by the Board of Education to be assigned to a Chicago high school, I asked the kids on the street about their local high school, and where it was located. They told me they went to Crane, but they couldn't tell me an address, so I drove around till I found it. I asked to be assigned to Crane and was hired.

At Crane I had total freedom to create my own curriculum and buy books (with my own money) for the classrooms. As a new teacher I'd been given the poorest students and their reading skills were very limited. I also had some very bright students who wanted to read and write. They really did not have safe locker spaces nor could they find a way to transport books around. So it was easiest for me to keep the books in safe spaces like my locker or a teacher's office, and bring them in on a cart. Occasionally, a principal would sit in class and observe me teach, but I never got any feedback, so I must have done all right.

I'd been asked by the principal to do the yearbook, and that meant often working late and then leaving school about 7:00 p.m. in the dark. Fortunately, across the street from Crane, was a rental parking lot where I'd gotten a space right next to the attendant's booth. He kindly waited until all the cars had left the lot, and then closed the gate. I was often the last one out. When I got home to Peoria Street, Barbara Gersmann, another volunteer, would be watching for me as I found a place to park and then walked home. Later, after Project House closed, I roomed with Hilda Carper in an apartment, and she watched out for me. The neighborhood was a red-light district, but fortunately I was never harmed.

Hilda Carper was a great stabilizing and caring presence in my life on Peoria Street. Besides doing the grocery shopping and cooking, Hilda made my wedding dress and organized the food for our wedding reception. She never complained when I moved out to get married, but invited her sister to join her.

I had visited Gail Piches Jackson, in St. Louis, who was living with her husband's family in the Black ghetto. There I observed up close how oppressive it was to live in segregation. This hit me hard and moved me to decide that I should participate with Martin Luther King Jr., and other civil rights leaders in the march from Selma to Montgomery, Alabama. This was serious; I accepted that we might get killed. The Alabama state troopers were definitely not there to protect us.

As a teacher I always tried to dress up, to look nice. On the ride to Selma with a few African-American pastors, they teased me about my bouffant hairdo and the big curlers I took along. Somewhere in Selma I realized I'd never have time to set my hair, so I threw all my curlers into a dumpster. I wanted a radically simple lifestyle to follow Jesus. I didn't want to look "attractive" anymore. Who was I trying to attract anyway? I was making more than a choice about hairstyles, fashions, and impressing people. I did not want to go back to the kind of life my parents hoped I'd live. In the context of poverty and the struggle for racial equality, I'd found my true self.

Allan Howe and I had been aware of each other during our time at Project House, but we never talked about our relationship. I thought he was too young for me since we were five years different. After Allan's two years at Project House were up and his alternative service time was over, I remember taking him to the train station so he could return to Los Angeles. I thought he was leaving for good, but then he let me know that he was coming back. I was glad.

By 1964, the West Side Christian Parish had closed down. Church of Hope on Peoria Street was the only church still going, but the Belsers had moved to Reba to recover their health. Only a small remnant remained. Allan Howe had started to attend Chicago Theological Seminary in Hyde Park, but once a week he returned to Church of Hope for an evening potluck and church meeting. I knew the dangers he faced returning by public transportation, so, since I had a car, I offered to drive him home, and that became a weekly date. Eventually this time together helped us see how alike we were in our beliefs and life goals. Our age difference no longer seemed to matter. On our rides back to Hyde Park, we'd stop and talk till midnight and beyond. We fell in love and decided to get married at Christmas rather than wait for the summer break. It was the most practical thing to do.

I called my mother and told her I was engaged. She asked, "Is he a Negro?" I paused for a long time to get my emotions under control, and then told her what she wanted to hear. "No, Mom," I said. "He's a blue-eyed blond from Pasadena, California." "Has he gone to college?" she asked. "Yes," I answered. "He's from Stanford." At that her questions stopped.

My mother was very worried about the cost of our wedding. However, the West Side Christian Parish had an office in the large First Congregational Church of Chicago, and that is why they let us use the building for free. Our wedding was on Christmas day, so they left all the decorations and flowers in place for our ceremony. It was hard to find a restaurant for the rehearsal dinner on Christmas Eve, but my parents found a lovely place in the Stock Yard Inn. It was all very reasonable. Allan's parents had more means to share and hosted a dinner at the Palmer House. Some of my students came to the wedding, and two of them were our ushers.

Allan and Jeanne newly married, surrounded by Allan's sister, Marcia, and his brother, Bruce

At our wedding my parents met Allan's folks, who invited them to come to California, where they promised a top-notch vacation. A couple of years later they did. Allan's parents dined and wined them up and down the West Coast. This was the happiest time of their lives, my parents said. They finally were enjoying the upper-middle-class lifestyle to which they'd always aspired. How ironic that their downwardly mobile children helped all that to happen! Allan had personally chosen a very frugal lifestyle on the West Side, and then he had to adjust to the gift of a new BMW as a wedding present from his parents. In fact, we were overwhelmed by the carloads of gifts mailed to us from friends of Allan's mother. Many of these gifts we gave away to Reba Place Fellowship or friends at Church of Hope in the weeks to follow. I was so overwhelmed, I asked for a month off of my teaching job after the wedding in order to send out thank-you notes, settle our new apartment in Hyde Park, and recover from exhaustion.

Meanwhile, on Peoria Street there were house fires all the time. People were leaving. The place was increasingly decimated. Rats roamed the streets boldly—homeless beggars. It was a hard time for rats and people. Our church was closing, our students were losing their school, our friends were scattering. The city had a grandiose plan to raze several square miles of degraded property to build huge, low-income apartment projects and the Chicago campus for the new University of Illinois. For us, however, this transition was a cause of deep grief.

I stayed friends with Rose Taylor, a mother in Church of Hope, who eventually ended up in the Robert Taylor Homes, one of the immense high-rise apartment buildings to house the poor. I visited her there a few times. The elevators were always broken. I climbed the stairs to the eleventh floor, passing gang members who probably would have robbed me but were too shocked to know what to do with a White woman in high heels. Rose always welcomed me and was most grateful for the little help I could offer her in desperate circumstances. We remained friends till her death. I kept up a similar relationship of visits to Fanny May Smith.

In February I had returned to teaching without our having time for a honeymoon vacation. So in June we drove to California in our BMW to visit Allan's folks. I'd never been west of Missouri. I was overwhelmed by Allan's parents' beautiful home. Their yard was way beyond any previous experience for me—a wide ranch house with a swimming pool in the back, complete with diving board. Palm trees lined the drive, mountains rose in the background, flowers grew everywhere, and fruit trees were dropping mangos, peaches, pomegranates, oranges, avocados, and cherries . . . I did not know what to make of it. Later on, when we had children, Allan's folks built a guest house so we could have a little more privacy on our visits. Allan's parents continued to lavish us with gifts, which was a tension for our new marriage. I was the one who wanted to relax and enjoy some of these gifts, eat out more often, while Allan was the principled frugal one who kept thinking of other people who needed these gifts and this money more than we did. We went his way.

IV. On to Elkhart, Indiana, Where We Tried and Failed at Christian Intentional Community

After Church of Hope, Allan wanted to study under John Howard Yoder, who was teaching theology at Associated Mennonite Biblical Seminaries in Goshen and Elkhart, Indiana. Hilda Carper knew the Yoders from her time of service in Europe, so she introduced us to their family. We ended up living just down the street from the Yoders and explored community with them. I taught high school in Elkhart for one year, and then our first son, Mark, was born. The Yoder girls were our babysitters. It was wonderful the way our families blended. However, the intentional Christian community we tried between the Yoders, Linds, and Howes did not take off. John was a social introvert and would not talk in meetings. After a time, the Linds went back to Reba. We started to attend one of the Mennonite churches, but all the thick family networks, history of denominational splits, and negotiations were always a mystery to me. After graduating from seminary, Allan taught elementary school one year, but it was not his forte.

V. We Rejoined the Belsers at Reba, Where We Learned Our Calling to Hospitality and Our Limits

So we moved back to Evanston, to Reba Place Fellowship, and into the Elmwood four-flat in order to live near Julius and Peggy Belser and their family. I found in Peggy the mother figure I had never had, and learned a lot about family life from the Belsers. With other Fellowship families at Elmwood (the Lehmans and the Browns) we had a strong family support system. That gave us courage to adopt two mixed-race children, Kathy and James Marcus.

But Elmwood was three blocks distant from the rest of the Fellowship. I told Allan I wanted to live nearer to the center of the action. Eventually, we ended up moving into a large house at 714 Reba Place. At that time, in the sixties and early seventies, many young people were looking for community and flocked to Reba. It was also a good time to buy houses as our neighborhood was turning over and property values had fallen. New buildings came up for sale just as we needed them.

Jeanne and Allan at Reba Park, still in love

Julius saw us as his protégés. People would arrive at the Belsers's household (the Clearing), which was already full, and he would ask us to take them in. During that time we rehabbed 714 Reba Place to finish the second floor and totally build out the third floor. Soon we had a dozen people living on top of our family of five. I was still learning how to be a mother. Finally, I burned out. The community arranged for others to take over leadership of the house.

For a couple of years, we lived at 712 Monroe, a two-bedroom apartment, and learned how to be a nuclear family, which was very healing. Then the large Warner family vacated 723 Seward Street and moved to help found Plow Creek Fellowship in the country two hours west of Chicago. Julius thought we should move in there and do hospitality on a more modest scale. This proved to be just right for our family. It worked well for our children and for a young single woman, Linda Kelsey, who lived with us for more than thirty years. She was a school counselor/social worker. She made her home with us since her parents were missionaries in Jordan.

The years living at 723 Seward were probably the best of my life. Our children grew up there and have many fond memories of those years. The house was big but still cozy. We could have the North Suburban Peace Initiative office there and not have Allan working long hours away from home. Later, when Allan was the missionary- and service-director of the Illinois Mennonite Conference, his office could be in the same basement space.

Our house at 723 Seward had a generous-sized kitchen and dining room where we could host as many as fourteen people around the table.

We often had homeless people show up at our door or hang out on our front porch. After a few years of this I learned that a woman who worked at the local South Boulevard El stop was referring them to us on some vague reputation that we cared for the poor. We got acquainted on the porch and with neighbors, and sometimes shared snacks, but this kind of hospitality never became a ministry for us.

VI. What Happened to Our Children?

Our oldest son, Mark, attended college at Goshen, Indiana, where he met his wife, Judy Woimanen, from the Upper Peninsula of Michigan. They married young, finished college, and moved to Chicago so Mark could attend law school at Loyola University. Judy worked as an accountant. After law school they moved to Green Bay, Wisconsin, where Mark began working in a law firm. Later, he went independent as a defender of folks caught in the criminal court system. They had two daughters, Colleen and Lily. They are all living in the Green Bay area including Colleen's husband, Dave and Judy's parents, and extended family.

Our daughter, Kathleen, lives in Seattle with her wife, Sarah, and their five children. Sarah has a well-paying job in computer advertising and Kathleen manages the children. (There are three teens now.) They live in a large home adjacent to a forest in Covington, Washington.

On November 27, 2013, we received a phone call from our daughter-in-law Danae from the hospital, telling us that she and Marcus had suffered an invasion of their Los Angeles home by robbers and that Marcus had died. The man who knocked on the door claimed to be raising money for children, and the other was hiding. When James opened the door, the knocker drew a gun and tried to force his way in, and the second gunman charged. James Marcus, who was strong, pushed the men out onto the porch and their guns into an upward position saying, "No!" Danae joined in the struggle to help Marcus. They called to their little son, just inside the door, to run and hide, which he did. Marcus was shot in the body, Danae in the pelvis, and then another shot to Marcus's head killed him. The robbers fled to their getaway car. We later learned that the robbers were gang members who had done many home invasions and had been brutal to other victims.

The devastation this caused our family has never ended, though we received wonderful support from so many people in California, Illinois, and all over. Beside the immensely moving and well-attended funeral, reception, and burial in Los Angeles, there was a memorial service for James Marcus at Reba. At both we saw friends from all over the country. James Marcus could not have been more beautifully remembered. At both, Danae sang and played piano in his honor, and their son, Sterling, was there. Julian Jackson made a slide show of James's life and showed it to all present. Danae survives, has good work, and is raising our grandson in a suburb of Seattle, the city where she grew up.

A few weeks later, and several home invasions after our son was killed, the robbers were caught because the LA Police and Northwestern LA suburban police departments had organized a mass response to any report of a home invasion in progress, in reaction to the highly publicized murder of James Marcus. Now, almost five years later, our family is still processing the grief, but the trial, conviction, and sentencing in 2018 were helpful. We're grateful to the LAPD for all their hard work. Despite the pain and grief, Allan and I sense the Lord with us.

VI. Why Have I Stayed on in Community at Reba?

Because the Lord led me to Church of Hope, to marriage with Allan, and then to Reba Place Fellowship, I have wanted to stay on and give back as I was able. For most of those years, I've been the office manager and receptionist of Reba Place Fellowship's central office, welcoming all who come and doing the tasks I can. The fact that Allan is now diagnosed with Lewy body disease doesn't change my commitments. We will walk together, day by day, hand in hand, praising God for his goodness to us, I hope, all the way to heaven.

Hospitality, Kindness, and Faithfulness

Linda Kelsey

Hospitality, kindness, and faithfulness are some of the qualities which come to mind when I think about dear Jeanne.

My first recollection of Jeanne was during a Sunday morning worship service at Reba Place Church, in 1981. She presented the Chom family with a photo album which she had developed, to commemorate the family's first year in the U.S. Jeanne was a point person when Reba Place Church sponsored the Chom family, the first of seven Cambodian refugee families who came to the U.S. through RPC. Jeanne assisted the Chom family as they transitioned to living in the U.S.

In 1982, I hoped to move into the Reba community, and was looking for a place to live. The Howe family invited me to stay in their home on an interim basis. I recall how their home immediately felt very cozy to me. My time living with the Howe family stretched out to twenty-nine years. It was such a comfort to have a place where I felt so much at home, since my parents lived across the ocean, in Jordan. Hospitality is embedded in the Arab culture and the missionary community in which I was raised. I knew that it would be exciting for me to again be around folk with whom extending hospitality was a way of life.

Over the years, many different persons lived with us in the Howes's home for weeks or years at a time. Jeanne and Allan are very committed to follow God's calling to Christians to extend hospitality. It seems to come so naturally to them, and I wanted to learn from them. The folks who stayed in their home came from Germany, South Africa, Tanzania, Ethiopia, China, Korea, Japan, Jordan, Panama, Canada, and the U.S.—as I remember it. The Howe family cherished having opportunities to learn about other cultures through their guests. Jeanne enjoyed taking folks on the CTA train to see downtown Chicago, or to go on a driving tour of places in Chicago where she had lived. Jeanne also graciously hosted family members and friends of those of us who were living in their home. Allan and Jeanne love celebrating special occasions over a meal. Some of those who moved into their home were in dire straits, and needed a place to stay while working on stabilizing their lives. Jeanne knew how to mentor. She prayed with folks and gave them timely practical support.

Jeanne has prepared tasty meals for hundreds of persons over the years! Cooking became a serious hobby for her. After perusing the kitchen cupboards, one of the young guests remarked: "Jeanne can make a nice meal out of nowhere!" Their table was custom built, long enough to accommodate fourteen persons. When additional space was needed, additional places were set up in the living room and on the porch. Jeanne hosted weekly small group meals at her home, for all the years they lived at 723 Seward. I feel grateful that I was able to participate in extending hospitality, by joining in the conversations during mealtime, and by giving some practical assistance.

Some who know Jeanne wonder how she has been able to create so many meals and provide overnight accommodations for so many folks. Jeanne cultivates her spiritual life through regular prayer and reading of Scriptures. This discipline deepens Jeanne's capacity to share love, joy, peace, and hope as she hosts guests. She regards her friends at the Clearing as models of persons who extend hospitality. Jeanne's excellent organizational skills also come into play. She prepares the bedrooms in advance, when possible. She has special systems for menu planning, shopping, and keeping her refrigerator organized. Jeanne knows how to stretch a modest budget. She generally does the prep work days prior to a big meal; she sets the table hours in advance. Jeanne is somewhat attached to her very efficient routines and systems, so it can be a struggle for her to share the kitchen with others.

Their home was a hub of social life for the Howe children, Mark, Kathleen, and James Marcus. During meals, Jeanne and Allan were intentional about giving each person at the table an opportunity to share about themselves or their day. Meal times were lively from the humor that everyone pitched in. For many years, Jeanne hosted some young adults with special needs for weekly meals. She prepared and delivered weekly meals to some elderly neighbors like Mama Grace and Dorothy Konsterlie. This went on for years. Most of those who were hosted by Jeanne had little to give in return, apart from friendship. And when the hospitality came to an end, the friendships continued. Some felt inspired to return for spontaneous visits, and Jeanne was always delighted to see them no matter how inconvenient the timing of their arrival.

Jeanne developed friendships with many of the children in the neighborhood, who came from families with limited resources. She facilitated experiences for them, such as leaf-raking jobs, parties, times in the gym at the Reba Church Ministry Center, and outings in Chicago. In the Crane High School on Chicago's West Side where Jeanne taught in the sixties, her students wrote their appreciation in the yearbook, and affirmed that she indeed merited the "Teacher of the Year" award. Jeanne has always had a gift for appropriate, encouraging words for those she encounters. She found joy in spotting items of used clothing which would be perfect for another person. When others erred, or neglected a responsibility, Jeanne consistently exercised patience and grace. She was deliberate in her forgiveness. Jeanne prays for those who took the life of her son beloved son, James Marcus.

Jeanne is faithful in all she does. She is faithful in her commitment to God through her lifestyle of simplicity and generosity. Jeanne is faithful to Allan, her cherished husband. Her faithfulness in recent months has included caring for Allan as he faces increasing disability. Jeanne has been very loyal to Reba Place Fellowship and Reba Place Church, of which she has been a member for nearly fifty years. She has been faithful in her relationships to her children, their spouses, her grandchildren, families of origin, and relatives. Jeanne is deeply committed to social justice and global peace. She participated in the march from Selma to Montgomery and countless demonstrations for peace. Jeanne has been faithful in caring for a variety of projects, ranging from cleaning the Reba Church Ministry Center to administering Sunday school for many years. When tasks are difficult or tiring, Jeanne perseveres, without complaining, and finishes the tasks well. She is attentive in caring for details.

Living with Jeanne for all these years gives me a close-in perspective. Her life embodies the Spirit of Christ as described in Galatians 5:22: "But the fruit of the Spirit is love, joy, peace, patience, kindness, goodness, faithfulness, gentleness and self-control." I am deeply enriched, like so many others who were blessed to receive Jeanne's love! It is my hope that I will continue to grow in passing on to others what I have received and learned.

Linda Kelsey's ode to Jeanne's faithfulness is matched now by her weekly provision of a Middle Eastern meal at the Howes's table. Linda is a social worker in the Chicago public school system.

"Embers ... Fall, Gall Themselves, and Gash Gold-Vermillion"

Heather Ashcroft Clark

Of the many moments Jeanne and I have talked together over the years, one conversation stands out in my mind as a rare gift. Jeanne had strained her back lifting a child, necessitating that she spend several days prone on the couch as she healed. I visited her, and we talked about her favorite poem, "The Windhover," written in 1877 by Gerard Manley Hopkins and dedicated "to Christ our Lord." Jeanne had committed it to memory for a literature class in college and recited it swiftly.

> **The Windhover**
> *To Christ our Lord*
>
> I caught this morning morning's minion, king-
>   dom of daylight's dauphin, dapple-dawn-drawn Falcon, in his riding
>   Of the rolling level underneath him steady air, and striding
> High there, how he rung upon the rein of a wimpling wing
> In his ecstasy! then off, off forth on swing,
>   As a skate's heel sweeps smooth on a bow-bend: the hurl and gliding
>   Rebuffed the big wind. My heart in hiding
> Stirred for a bird,—the achieve of, the mastery of the thing!
>
> Brute beauty and valour and act, oh, air, pride, plume, here
>   Buckle! AND the fire that breaks from thee then, a billion
> Times told lovelier, more dangerous, O my chevalier!
>
>   No wonder of it: shéer plód makes plough down sillion
> Shine, and blue-bleak embers, ah my dear,
>   Fall, gall themselves, and gash gold-vermillion.[1]

---

1. https://www.poetryfoundation.org/articles/69191/gerard-manley-hopkins-the-windhover.

A Hopkins lover myself, I savored the chance to linger over these lines and images so meaningful for Jeanne and learn the wisdom she'd taken from them.

As the poem begins, Hopkins thrills to the wild perfection of the airborne falcon. Then with the word "buckle," he brings the poem plummeting earthward to the "sheer plod" of a farmer walking behind a plow, turning over the soil. Jeanne drew my attention to that verb on which the whole poem turns, explaining that, in order for Christ's character to be formed in us, reliance on our native gifts and abilities (imaged by the bird's mastery of flight) must buckle and give way to plodding daily submission to the work of loving God and neighbor. Only then will what flames forth from our lives be dangerous to the principalities and powers of this world.

How did this movement show up in Jeanne's story? How did she buckle? And what has flamed forth?

Jeanne's story (as recorded here and in a previously published interview) reveals several significant "pressure points"—growing up a latchkey kid in a lonely home with parents who urged her toward upward mobility, witnessing the suffering caused by economic and social disparity between different races, struggling with depression and a sense of hopelessness as she moved into her later twenties with increasing dysfunction in her family of origin and a failed romantic relationship. At a point of extreme internal pressure, Jeanne buckled; she cried out to God to reveal himself. Soon thereafter, she remembered a classmate who had spoken of Project House and decided to make an inquiry. What she found there gave her a sense that God was present in that place and the people gathered there.

Once settled at Project House with the West Side Christian Parish, Jeanne plunged in a direction of downward mobility, taking a teaching job in an underresourced, inner-city school, using her own funds to provide books for her students. She put herself in physical danger living in a ghetto neighborhood and in making a trip to the march in Selma in a van with two Black pastors and another White woman. She met Allan, a Stanford graduate "born with a silver spoon in his mouth," and the two of them put their hands to the plow.

Hopkins, speaking of the "sheer plod" of the life of submitted discipleship, uses the term "sillion," the thick slice of soil turned over by the plow to lie glinting with minerals in the sun. In medieval times, sillion denoted a small strip of ground granted to monasteries to farm. Jeanne found in the Reba neighborhood her field to plow, sowing seeds of faith and humble service. In the early seventies, one seed multiplied in a half-hour PBS documentary on RPF, featuring Jeanne as a young mother living in household and articulating her vision of community. During my own season of young motherhood, Jeanne has brought me food, cleaned my house, watched my children, urged me to buy decent shoes, and encouraged me in moments of conversation snatched in my stairwell and during hours of listening and prayer in small groups. Standing on my second-floor balcony, I've watched her go down the street picking up trash, sweeping up broken glass, calling less-privileged neighbors by name. She made sheer plod shine.

Getting back to "The Windhover," the poem takes a final turn to the image of seemingly spent embers that, in the act of falling and breaking apart, reveal the fire still burning at their core. The one who puts her hand to the plow and does not turn back learns that her God is indeed "a consuming fire." Letting this love fuel the flame of her life, Jeanne has spent herself here in community, embracing its gifts and disappointments. In recent years, she's persevered through the trauma of their younger son's murder and the Lewy body dementia that has dimmed Allan's flame. Jeanne's love burns steadily in attentive accompaniment of her valiant plowing partner, the new plod of her days. She continues to inspire me. In her falling, I glimpse gold-vermillion.

~

Heather Clark is a playful wordsmith and poet, a mentor of younger women in the Reba community, and experienced in community leadership. She is married to philosopher Greg Clark and is the mother of two young adult sons.

EIGHT

Concluding Reflections

Priceless Treasure in Cracked Pots

DAVID JANZEN

We have just read the life stories of seven idealistic young adults who, despite burnout and disillusionment, persevered to become radical elders for another generation. We've also reviewed the testimony of a small cloud of witnesses who assess the impact of these seven mentors and community leaders. Time has come now to sum up the wisdom that they, and we, have glimpsed by means of some concluding reflections. But what we see will depend on where we stand and what kind of wisdom we are looking for.

Six times in Matthew's Sermon on the Mount, Jesus compares two kinds of wisdom: "You have heard that it is said, . . ." contrasts with "But I say to you, . . ." For example, "You have heard that it is said, 'You shall love your neighbor and hate your enemy.' But I say to you, 'Love your enemy and do good to those who persecute you'" (5:43). We might call these two life paths "conventional wisdom" and the "wisdom of the kingdom," or looking at its defining moment, the "wisdom of the cross."

When Jesus called his disciples, he asked them to leave family and professions behind, moving from life story A (before Jesus) to life story B with Jesus as the Messiah in whom they put their hope for an Israel restored to sovereignty. Jesus's crucifixion utterly crushed these dreams. Disillusioned, they contemplated returning to Galilee, to the life of conventional wisdom they had known, an A—B—A kind of story. However, the resurrected Jesus appeared among them in mysterious yet familiar form, and instructed them to wait in Jerusalem for power to carry on his mission. When the Spirit descended at Pentecost and the church was born, they rejoiced to realized that they were entering into an A—B—C kind of life in which the Spirit would guide them. Now they had the power to carry on the reconciling mission of Jesus in service to the church community and to the ends of the earth. This was the kingdom coming that Jesus had promised.

The memoirs of seven elders whose lives we have followed closely thus far, are they A—B—A stories of disillusionment and return to an easier status quo? Or are they A—B—C stories that, following disillusioned idealism, embody the wisdom of the cross as we see it unfolding in the New Testament? Let's return to the six questions we posed in the Preface, and see what insights they might open up.

I. On Leaving and Finding

Jesus promised his followers that by leaving behind family and possessions for the kingdom's sake, they would receive back a hundredfold in this life, along with persecutions and life eternal (Matt 19:29; Mark 10:30). How do the life experiences of these seven prophets fit with Jesus's promise?

For each of these seven young people personal relationships were a crucial bridge in their conversion stories. John Betten, a coworker and interviewer for this *Seven Radical Elders* book, commented,

> Hilda meets John Miller in Switzerland who is married into her family and who becomes a founder of Reba Place Fellowship. Peggy works with Dan West, a Church of the Brethren peace-movement organizer. A friend in an interracial marriage inspired Jeanne to take on the March from Selma to Montgomery. In every case, a strong friendship pointed the way in the radical changes they made. The younger generation of readers should remember that close relationships are needed both for radical conversion and for sustaining those radical commitments through the decades of one's life.

These relationships made a connection to a new spiritual family. Jesus's creation of spiritual families was not meant to do away with blood families, but it was a way of stretching family to include all whose first desire was to do God's will. By renouncing personal possessions and (in some cases, giving away inheritances), these seven young radicals found a new spiritual family that offered stronger support for following Jesus than they could have known in conventional nuclear families like their parents'.

Jeanne Casner Howe had many tensions with her mother's fashion-conscious, upwardly-mobile aspirations. Early on, she identified with an African-American house maid who, though economically poor, was rich in the Christian virtues of faith, hope, and love. At the point where Jeanne began to pursue her own life directions in college, valuing interracial, working-class friendships more than sorority peers, her mother cut off financial support. Casting in her lot with the West Side Christian Parish strained the family ties even more.

Allan Howe's competitive and ambitious streak was cheered on by a grandfather who had him pegged to become president of the United States. But when teenage Allan learned about pacifism from a Methodist friend, he undertook a thorough study of the New Testament and began to argue (competitively, of course) for a pacifist stance. He soon got into long debates with his father and uncle, who had military backgrounds to defend. Though there were continual tensions between the wealthy Howe parents and the frugal Allan, who kept giving his inheritance away to others more in need, the relationship with family never actually broke down. In her later years, Allan's mother commended him for his faithful service as a Christian minister and credited him with changing her mind about many things like race relations and peacemaking.

The tensions with parents over radical lifestyle choices were not as pronounced for Julius, Peggy, Hilda, Albert, and Margaret, perhaps because their parents were of rural Anabaptist (Church of the Brethren and Mennonite) stock. Their churches were already involved in counter-cultural commitments to pacifism and community—albeit of a more tidy, middle-class sort. Peggy tells how uncomfortable her parents were to visit them in the West Side Chicago ghetto, and how much they cried when Julius and Peggy returned to that mission calling. But their relationships stayed strong out of familial loyalty and shared commitment to the way of Jesus.

So, did Jesus's promise of a hundredfold restoration of what had been sacrificed come true? Of course, these seven young prophets did not enter into these sacrifices based upon a calculation of a financial return on investment. There was no spreadsheet keeping track of friends and houses according to Jesus's metaphorical promise. But decades later, these seven elders would agree that the new family they received in Christian community, and in friendships with the poor, increased their trust in Jesus and his promise. Their network of communities and friends goes on and on. After some initial mistakes at Church of Hope and Reba Place Fellowship, the all-things-in-common community and family life found a more healthy and sustainable balance such that the children of community are grateful, not just for the love they've received, but for the example of sacrificial service that they inherited. The loyalty of their physical and spiritual children, grandchildren, and great-grandchildren has multiplied this gift to the seven radical elders and their community.

The sweetest example, perhaps, of Jesus's words of promise coming true might be found in the stories of Hilda Carper's mother and Julius Belser's parents, who chose to live out the last years of their lives in the Clearing Household, under the roof and care of their children, supported by a loving and grateful community.

As we grow old in community and pass on from this life to the next, Jesus's promise makes sense in one more way. Those who give up home and family for Jesus's sake are promised not just persecutions, but also eternal life. These seven elders have come to see that communities of radical hospitality not only bring heaven to earth, but the promise of eternal life already begins here and now because it participates on earth in the justice and the peace that is heaven.

II. After Disillusionment, What Remains?

What illusions did these idealists have to shed, and what remained of their original vision? In what ways did they remain radical disciples of Jesus to the end of their days?

Let's begin with the observation that disillusionment is a good thing. If we are, in fact, carrying illusions, the sooner we know it and leave them behind, the better. Right?

We sometimes disparage the ideals of youth because they often do not last. In the case of these seven young radicals, their ideals, however naïve, did have a positive provisional role in their discipleship development. Young people are often oriented and motivated by ideals because they have little experience of God's faithfulness in the nitty-gritty of life. The ideals of these seven radicals carried them into a discipleship community, into service on the West Side of Chicago, into improbable friendships across race and class lines. These ideals got them to meet poor and disadvantaged people in relationships that, though sometimes superficial, did have the power to begin the genuine work of transformation. Idealism can lift young people into a life of sacrificial service and, for a time, the "honeymoon" experience of loving freely and giving generously feels heroic and immediately rewarding, enough to move life from stage A to stage B.

When Allan Howe threw himself into West Side ward politics and organized others to campaign for a reform aldermanic candidate, his heart was crushed by how easily the mob boss's corruption stole the election. Allan realized his hopes in idealized civics-textbook democracy had been misplaced. The steep and patient work of building an interracial community of Jesus-followers became more credible. Allan recalls his own transforming moment when an African-American sister walked out of the community meeting two times because she was afraid of White people. And two times she came back to share her grief and receive comfort over her son going back to prison. If this woman's faith was that strong and that real, he too wanted to throw his lot in with this tribe, following Jesus together wherever he might lead.

Peggy Belser tells about her disillusionment when she learned that poverty and racial prejudice are much more deeply rooted in traumatized souls and in entrenched social systems than she first imagined. Her efforts to model good, middle-class virtues were not sufficient to help her poverty-stricken neighbors to break out of their plight. Even though there were genuine breakthroughs in relationships between Blacks and Whites, when the Church of Hope was erased from the West Side map by urban renewal, none of the African-American members made the move to Evanston with the White members.

We could rehearse more such stories, but if you have read the seven memoirs, you can give your own examples. In their experience of shattered ideals these seven radicalized young people found the treasure of a new solidarity with one another and with Jesus, who was mysteriously present in the painful joy of vulnerable and honest relationships. The naïve ideals served a divine purpose both for the disciples of Jesus and the seven radical young prophets of our story. They brought people together close enough that a transforming fusion reaction could take place.

At this point an analysis of how to suffer well might be helpful. There are three responses we can make to suffering: flee it, fix it, or face it.

We might flee suffering by seeking distractions, finding comfort in addictions, or indulging in denial, for example.

However, if we are privileged with resources, we might try to fix the causes of suffering by various do-gooder techniques. This is both good and loving, but it is usually only a partial solution. Peggy Belser believed that the positive example of middle-class virtues would be enough for her ghetto friends to overcome poverty. She believed that good intentions could overcome the hurt of racism. Allan Howe thought that political organizing could fix corrupt politics. Such illusions were crucified by stubborn reality. That is usually enough for most idealists to flee from their suffering to the more sheltered life they had come from.

However, something more miraculous happened. These White idealists and their Black friends in the Church of Hope stuck around and suffered together, with the result that a fierce loyalty grew up between them. They tasted something real that was more valuable than anything the world had to offer. When they came to the end of their own strength, they discovered the presence of Jesus resurrected among them, bonding them together for what turned out to be the rest of their lives. These lessons of suffering well, learned first on Chicago's West Side, continued at Reba Place Fellowship, as we shall see, in their experience of burnout and restoration.

III. On Burnout and Restoration

In these memoirs we see that Julius Belser, Allan Howe, and Albert Steiner, each at about the age of thirty, got carried away by grandiose ministry commitments such that their marriages and families almost fell apart. It is crucial to notice that turning a man's ambitions toward a holy cause does not necessarily redeem that ambition.

After six years at Church of Hope on Chicago's West Side, Peggy felt overwhelmed with hospitality demands, their children were not thriving, and Julius was seldom available because of his care for other needy people. Peggy feared that if she unloaded all her needs, Julius would leave her. For years they had been running on parallel paths without deep and honest sharing of souls. When Peggy emotionally broke down and, as it were, went on strike, Reba leaders intervened and encouraged Julius and Peggy to take a sabbatical in Evanston, where they would have minimal responsibilities and time to deepen communication in their marriage and care for their struggling children. This did not mean abandoning their call to racial integration and social justice, but it was a judicious rebalancing of life with more community support in a common purse, so that the radical call of

Jesus could be sustained for the rest of their years. Eventually they committed to take off Tuesdays each week for a day away from community cares to listen to each other and get reconnected in patient communication.

With Allan and Jeanne Howe, the breakdown came a few years later at Reba when the community was at the height of the charismatic renewal's influence. At that time almost everyone was living in large, extended, ministering households. Many needy and broken persons flocked to Reba for the support they hoped to receive in an intensive communal life. More and more newcomers were added to Toad Hall till there were eighteen persons sharing a common table with Allan, Jeanne, and their children. Meanwhile, Allan was in over his head, counseling troubled souls and tracking multiple meetings each week about community governance. Jeanne bore with this until one day she unloaded in an elder's meeting, pouring out her overwhelmed feelings in an epic cry for help. As a result, the Howes were relieved of most responsibilities and eventually moved into an apartment of their own for a season of healing. Though it felt like a punitive exile at the time, the faithful connection with Julius and Peggy Belser carried them through to better days. Eventually, Allan gained enough pastoral care experience to make more mature decisions about how much ministry they could sustain. At the same time (1979–1980), the community went through a period of review where leadership confessed to serious mistakes of judgment, resulting in a sober reassessment of the Reba culture that had overdosed on authority. This led to a more modest but sustainable way for Allan and Jeanne to host an extended family household at 723 Seward, an arrangement that blessed them and their guests for almost thirty years. On that stronger communal foundation with more mature leadership, Reba Place Fellowship entered into a generation-long season of relative peace, balancing inner healing and outward engagement according to the gifts of the people sharing life.

Similarly, Albert Steiner, found himself overextended in a full-time outside job, plus committee meetings and managerial responsibilities in the Fellowship, that left his wife, Carol, starved of the "softer side" of marriage. With the encouragement of other community leaders, Albert rebalanced his commitments and entered into a more intentional healing journey with Carol. This helped Albert discover his own path of intimacy with God, who became the source of healing for his own shattered self-esteem.

We could add other similar stories to this litany. But they all beg the question of how to account for the amazing resilience that can admit

Concluding Reflections

mistakes and exhaustion, receive help and healing, and yet gracefully persist over seven lifetimes of service. We don't see all the details of these healing journeys, but we do see that the adjustments made over time with community discernment arrived at a balance of needs and resources that made ministry, marriage, and family life sustainable for the long haul, befitting a more long-term assessment of everyone's gifts. In this A—B—C pattern of life, "C" might stand for "communally discerned Holy Spirit guidance over the long haul." This path also leads through an increased capacity for suffering well, resulting in increasing joy and holiness of life, which we will explore in the last section of this "Concluding Reflections" essay.

IV. The Racial Reconciliation Impact of Seven Radical Elders on Their Communities

I asked Anne Stewart to help me evaluate the impact of the "seven radical elders" at Reba and Plow Creek in the direction of racial reconciliation. But as we talked, it became clear that Anne, herself, belongs at the center of this story.

Anne Stewart is an African-American grandma who just celebrated her eightieth birthday. She would also qualify as one of Reba's radical elders, but one who came by a different route than the Chicago West Side/Church of Hope connection. Before joining Reba Place Fellowship, Anne taught African-American literature in high school in an era when such a college major, such an academic niche, and even such textbooks did not yet exist. For a decade she "made it happen" until she had three children. Other friends were headed toward Reba Place Fellowship and she joined them. This was in the 1970s.

For a few years Anne's family lived at Plow Creek to get her oldest son, Kenny, away from gang influence. This move and Plow Creek community "saved my life," Kenny now claims.

Back at Reba, sometime around 1986, Julius Belser and Anne Stewart teamed up to pioneer some changes in the Fellowship and church, to make Reba feel more "at home" for African Americans who were by then a majority of the neighborhood. "What would happen," Anne asked, "if we had Black leadership in the church, Black music, and everyone was exposed to anti-racism training?" Julius's response was, "Let's try and see how it goes." They were clear that both personal relationships and social structures needed to change.

Anne is humble about her first attempts at anti-racism training at Reba where she and coleader Mary Pat Martin at first assumed that "if it doesn't go well, it is 'them,' rather than 'us,' the teachers." However, despite some guilt trips and tense reactions, over time more interracial friendships grew, as did the learning that comes from more honest listening by Whites to the experience of African Americans as peers.

Black music at Reba caught on, especially as embodied in an interracial Black gospel choir. By now (2019), with Anne's son, Kenny, in the middle of the music group, we witness a multicultural worship style that is at home with the resources of the African-American heritage. Anne herself leads the offertory most Sundays with a spiritual from her growing up days in Mississippi.

However, the imported Black leadership experiment at Reba Place Church did not last long. Looking back at that era, Anne concludes that tackling both race and gender issues at the same time was too much. A good number of members left the church at this time of heightened tensions. But Reba Place Fellowship, with its intentional community commitment, was rooted in the neighborhood, and not leaving. Around this communal core, plus a few other stalwart families and individuals, Reba Place Church made a new beginning that has carried on, incorporating the gifts of women and people of color as a matter of course.

At the height of those tensions, Anne reports, "I responded by being gone for ten years, pursuing a career in anti-racism training with Cross-Roads. When I came back," she observes, "I was surprised to see that many changes had taken place and that I felt welcome again. Also, the way we did racial reconciliation training had changed quite a bit, focusing more on institutional change. These institutions were created by White people for White people, not with the purpose of keeping others out, but despite good intentions, that was the effect. Over time, we became more skillful at what we were doing in these training sessions, and organizations were willing to pay us to do it. It takes hard work, we discovered, and persistent collaboration between people of color and Whites to dismantle and reconstruct institutions to make this deeper reconciliation happen."

These days Anne is grateful that the people in Reba Church "let me be who I am, let me be myself. I get people to sing my music, and that gives me joy."

So, what has been the general impact of these seven radical elders on their communities in the direction of racial reconciliation? One way of

Concluding Reflections

summarizing this impact is that their radical formation at Church of Hope has continued in a "preferential option" for relationships with people of color, with the poor, and those on the margins.

In retrospect, it was naïve on the part of Whites at the Church of Hope to imagine that their leadership plus good intentions could give birth to a sustainable interracial community where people had equal investment and authority.

From 1971 to 2017 Plow Creek Fellowship, in rural, conservative (and often racist) western Illinois, stood out as an odd community with a few interracial marriages, some interracial adoptions, and a steady stream of refugees coming through as workers and as visitors from sister community Valle Nuevo in El Salvador. Anne Stewart's story tells about their radical hospitality to her family in need of sanctuary. Pastor Rich Foss characterized Plow Creek as a "global village seeking the peace of Jesus." Margaret Gale played an important role in explaining and smoothing over these neighborhood tensions with the many friends she had made in the town of Tiskilwa.

Over the years, Reba Place Fellowship has usually had a few people of color in its membership, representing long-term friendships, intermarriage, or adoptions. But no minority male leaders have joined the community long-term. Anne Stewart and others have observed that most Whites who chose the downward path of intentional community do so having had the option of higher paying careers or generational wealth, or they came from families where simple living was a virtue, not a necessity. For African-American young adults who have never known the American dream, and who have been alienated by working under White leadership, intentional community is a harder choice.

Reba came to understand that if you want a diverse intentional community, you need to begin with reconciled leadership diversity from its foundation. That was not going to happen retroactively at Reba Place Fellowship, but it could happen in the next generation, as it were, with individuals and ministries that its members helped to launch.

In the 1980s RPF sent mission partners Richard and Ruth Anne Friesen to south Texas, sharing a high-stress life with Central American refugees on their way to asylum in Canada and the U.S.

Currently, Chico and Tatiana Fajardo-Heflin are in mission to the south-Chicago African-American suburb of Ford Heights, where endemic poverty and crime make raising a family highly dangerous. Instead of paternalistically launching social change programs, Chico and Tatiana have majored in friendships, local church participation, and foster-parenting a couple of teenagers. They discovered that this suburb, though abandoned by empire, has many people of faith and is in no way abandoned by God.

Reba Day Nursery (now Reba Early Learning Center) was launched by Hilda Carper and a few volunteers, but soon grew into its own building and began to hire teachers of color to connect better with the children who were coming. After Hilda "graduated" from leadership, Allan Howe became the chairman of the board for the rest of his active years, overseeing the hiring of an African-American director and assistant director. The resources from both Black and White communities flow in to support this thriving ministry involving fifty preschool children and a dozen staff members.

Reba Properties and Reba Place Development Corporation are parallel organizations developing and sustaining affordable housing. Julius's son Nevin, who grew up thinking he was Black like his friends on the Chicago West Side, for many years now has been director of Reba Properties. Nevin oversees a highly diverse and capable staff that has made Reba buildings some of the most desirable and affordable places to live in Evanston and northern Chicago.

Alongside this operation, Julius Belser (Nevin's father) as chairman of the board nurtured Reba Place Development Corporation in a direction that could access government funding for properties that required greater subsidies to stay affordable. RPDC is now led by its second African-American executive director. Both staff and leadership of these organizations are integrated in a way that resembles the make-up of the residents in the two hundred housing units they manage in both Evanston and the Rogers Park neighborhood of Chicago.

The most diverse organization that grew from Reba roots is Living Water Community Church, planted two miles south of the Reba Evanston enclave, in the Rogers Park neighborhood of Chicago. At the time when many members left Reba Place Church in the early nineties, some went back to White congregations. But others began a new congregation with a communal core that included Black (Carl McKinney) and White (Sally Schreiner Youngquist) co-pastors from the beginning. This congregation is now larger than its mother church, with a majority membership of minorities, many of them immigrants from Congo, Nepal, Cambodia, and other sources. They all worship together, and then worship in their distinctive language groups as well. Some of us imagine that this colorful mix of languages, cultures, music, food, and dance is a foretaste of the reconciliation of all things in Christ that we will know in heaven.

Not everyone is gifted as innovators of interracial nonprofit organizations and ministries like Julius, Hilda, Allan, and their next generation of disciples. But interracial friendships and extended-household living arrangements have characterized Reba Place Fellowship, fostering a community culture that has transformed the broader church life.

Anne Stewart summarized her appreciation for the impact for social change of the seven radical elders: "They kept learning from their mistakes, and there was that thing in them that did not quit." So, what is "that thing in them that did not quit?" This is the theme of our next essay on commitment.

V. The Necessity and the Freedom of Commitment

In our hyper-individualistic age, commitment is a radically subversive form of resistance.

Wendell Berry writes perceptively about the long-term gift of fidelity in marriage and community:

> What marriage offers—and what fidelity is meant to protect—is the possibility of moments when what we have chosen and what we desire are the same. Such a convergence obviously cannot be continuous. No relationship can continue very long at its highest emotional pitch. But fidelity prepares us for the return of these moments, which give us the highest joy we can know; that of union, communion, atonement (in the root sense of at-one-ment).[1]

Berry's comment suggests that we should make life commitments when there is an alignment between what we choose knowing it is best for others, and what we desire for ourselves. Our desires may change with our emotions and circumstances, but our choice before God and our covenant community carries us through hard slogging until we learn from our failures and arrive at wisdom gained by suffering well.

Commitment to Jesus and community for these seven radicals and their travel companions over time has not been a once-and-forever decision that shuts down all further thought in blind obedience. Commitment creates a space where we share our needs and our dreams in honest conversation, but we do not expect to have the last word. The last word belongs

---

1. Wendell Berry, "The Body and the Earth," in *The Art of the Commonplace: The Agrarian Essays* (Washington, DC: Counterpoint, 2002), 117.

to a God who hears our deepest needs and desires, and who loves us more than we can imagine. The mysterious presence of the Holy Spirit is revealed in free individuals being led together into a common purpose that everyone can accept as good news. As with marriage, a commitment to community is a decision to let the hardships of life take us deeper in the same direction rather than spread ourselves thin among all of life's options. And that is where we find the communion, the "at-one-ment" which Wendell Berry describes as the highest joy humans can know.

I remember speaking once with a group of young people exploring community who, like their millennial peers, were wary of commitment. I compared their generation's affliction to a farmer who digs ten wells three feet deep and wonders why he has not struck water. The young man sitting in front of me raised his hand and acknowledged, "Guilty as charged." Commitment is an acknowledgement that our lifetimes are finite, and trying to know everything before we commit is to know nothing deeply. In this life we never get to start from some ideal "scratch." The best we can do in our search for truth is to begin by acting on the truth that we know, trusting that this obedience will lead us through failure to greater truth, to a deeper understanding of God's will. This fruitful journey of doing the truth stops when our ego, our false self, attaches to partial truth as if our lives depended upon it.

The Reba Place Fellowship covenant does not assume we will always be at Reba. Our larger commitment is to the kingdom of God as embodied in Jesus and his call. So, there is always the possibility that we might be called by God to serve in another community setting or another mission where our gifts and needs align more fruitfully. However, we are not going to discern this alone, but with the help of our sisters and brothers who seek God's will too.

Jeanne Howe, who grew up in a dysfunctional family, is so grateful that her husband, Allan, has stayed committed to Reba, so that she could do so too with an undivided heart. Hilda Carper is surprised that here, in her nineties, she is still at Reba. Several times she tested another call, but it never panned out, so here she remains. But testing those other calls has given her the joy of knowing she is at Reba voluntarily in obedience to God's leading, which is her deepest desire.

Commitment is not a trap, not a shutting down of one's mind, not a stifling of desire. It is the discovery that within marriage, within a community, a whole new world opens up. The narrow wardrobe door opens

Concluding Reflections

out into a new and wondrous country called Narnia, hidden and yet open for exploration of wonders. The hidden treasure Jesus promises is found by selling all and investing in Jesus's future with a whole heart. As Kyle Mabb writes in his essay of appreciation for Julius Belser,

> Young Christians need to know that this is possible, that we can pour ourselves out on the altar of Christian service and receive the grace that rejuvenates us again and again. We need to see someone who's made mistakes, gotten burned, hurt others, asked for forgiveness, and above all, kept going.

We can make arguments from Scripture or from first principles about the blessings of a radical commitment to Jesus, to the poor, to those God has given us to love in community. Conventional wisdom can always come up with counterarguments. But as these stories of *Seven Radical Elders* demonstrate, there is no refutation to a life that has learned to suffer well and come through to joy.

VI. On Becoming Who We Were Meant to Be—Saints

We are uneasy talking about sainthood, and yet the New Testament assumes this is the destiny of those who follow Jesus. At the risk of sounding naïve, I want to propose that the radical path to sainthood is simple: it is learning from Jesus how to carry to God our own pain (and the pain of others) in the living flesh of our own souls, rather than inflicting this pain on others. There are in this world many hidden saints, people who bear the sins of the world along with Jesus. There are a few public saints who happen to be teachers and mentors of this way of life, and so may end up in books. But the ones who are written about and the ones who die in obscurity count the same in the kingdom of God. In some ways writing this book has been easy because the seven elders portrayed in it are beyond caring about their reputations. Such ego entanglements are for us more sophisticated folks at the beginning of the journey who are still learning to suffer well enough to experience the blessing of the pure in heart who will see God.

The essays of appreciation that follow these memoirs sometimes read like hagiography, like admiring stories of the saints who look faultless when viewed from afar. But they also include realistic portraits of the crackpots and the cracked pots that contain the priceless treasure of faithful lives that keep growing in the virtues of Jesus. The lives of these "saints" are not finished projects. When you read closely, you can see that their pursuit of holiness is not boring at all. Over time they have become more eccentric, more interesting, more free to be authentically themselves.

Newcomers to a closely shared life in community soon find their faults exposed to common knowledge. It takes them a little longer to realize that those who see their faults love them anyway. After decades in the rock tumbler of community, these saints are actually a joy to live with. They have developed habits of looking out for others as well as themselves. They apologize easily when they discover that someone is hurt by their words or actions. They have all learned something from Julius and from Jesus about how to live secure in God's unfailing love, which allows the work of reconciliation to go forward without time and energy wasted in defending one's own ego. These saints have learned how to skillfully speak the truth so that after you have been corrected, you still feel embraced. They are content to not have the last word, but to trust the authority of their experience and the inner conviction of the Holy Spirit to say what needs to be said. One gift the seniors in community can offer in times of trouble is to say, "We've been here before. We've seen worse than this, and God has brought us through."

Holiness has at its root a vision of wholeness, where all the parts fit together the way God intended. Holiness/wholeness has a simple core and yet is complex enough to connect all the parts. It is not something that can be forced, but that happens organically over time. Some Bible commentators have noticed that the Beatitudes are like scaling a mountain where peacemaking is the summit, a climb we are invited to make with Jesus, who has been there and done that before us. These seven radical elders, though in no way perfected, have persevered on a journey of faithful witness to the inexhaustible source of justice and peace available to this world in God's love.

The holiness of Jesus unifies both the personal and social dimensions of life. Holiness in each of these seven persons has been nurtured, as Linda Kelsey writes, in personal practices of "prayer, and reading of Scripture, and [a] lifestyle of simplicity and generosity." Each of these exemplars practices some version of "listening to the Lord" for guidance and for courage to follow up on what has been revealed. Instead of settling for a shallow, conventional life of avoiding pain and maximizing happiness, these faithful witnesses have persisted in the hidden work of service and suffering with others that finds joy in what is real. This is where the long journey that began with idealism and passed through disillusionment has led to—the most radical realism that humans can know because of the love of God in Christ Jesus. This is the inner side of holiness—communion with God who loves, challenges, guides, and never abandons us, even in times of crucifixion.

This deeper soul work also has the power to transform the world. These seven elders have discovered the secret of social holiness, that faithfully pursues the wholeness of reconciled relationships, that creatively acts for justice by persistent and nonviolent means, that lays down personal possessions and life goals meant to satisfy "just me" while remaining passionate in the quest for a common good. Because these lives are not motivated by the usual perks of privilege, and cannot be manipulated by the fear of death, from their "plodding hidden labor of loving and serving neighbor" a flame springs forth which is radically "dangerous to the principalities and powers of this world."[2] They demonstrate the good news that Jesus talked about in the Sermon on the Mount, a light that shines in the darkness, a city on a hill, an alternative community that does not compute by the motivations of conventional wisdom and that beckons as an inspiring real-life option for the next generation.

2. See Heather Ashcroft Clark's essay of appreciation for Jeanne Howe.

A Brief Chronology of the Seven Radical Elders' Story

Church of Hope	Reba Place Fellowship
Church of Hope	**Reba Place Fellowship**
Dates of Birth: 3-4-1927, Hilda Carper 9-12-1929, Peggy Eberley Belser 3-15-1931, Julius Belser 4-11-1935, Margaret Wenger Gale 12-20-1935, Albert Steiner 4-21-1937, Jeanne Casner Howe 2-5-1942, Allan Howe	1957 Reba Place Fellowship opens 1959–66, a strong partnership grows between Church of Hope and Reba 1965 Belsers move to Reba 1966 Hilda, Albert, and Gales move to Reba
1959 Church of Hope opened 1965 Belsers take a "sabbatical" 1966 Church of Hope closes	1969 Howes come to Reba after three years in Elkhart, IN 1969, John and Louise Miller, Reba co-founders, move to Canada. A younger generation takes charge at Reba. Virgil Vogt, John Lehman, and Julius Belser are senior elders for thirty years.
Plow Creek Fellowship 1970 Reba purchases a run-down farm in Bureau County, IL. Plow Creek Fellowship begins as a Reba annex. 1973 Plow Creek stands on its own feet, no longer a Reba subsidiary 1980s Plow Creek has peak membership of about forty-five persons . . . . . 2016–17, within two months three Plow Creek Elders pass away: Jim Harnish, David Gale, and Rich Foss 2017 Plow Creek closes operations, giving most of the land and all the buildings to a new nonprofit called Hungry World Farm	1970, Reba sends first pioneers to Plow Creek Farm 1970s, Charismatic Renewal transforms community life and worship at Reba, and eventually at Plow Creek, too 1980, Reba review opens a congregational option. Reba Place Church begins as a separate organization. . . . . . December 19, 2018, Julius Belser dies. July 2, 2019, Allan Howe dies.

www.ingramcontent.com/pod-product-compliance
Lightning Source LLC
Chambersburg PA
CBHW020839160426
43192CB00007B/714